MW01658167

Sixth Edition

THE MICHIGAN NOTARY LAW PRIMER

All the hard-to-find information every Michigan Notary Public needs to know!

National Notary Association

Published by:

National Notary Association
9350 De Soto Ave.
Chatsworth, CA 91311-4926
Telephone: (818) 739-4000
Fax: (818) 700-0920
Website: www.NationalNotary.org
Email: nna@nationalnotary.org

The information in this *Primer* is correct and current at the time of its publication, although new laws, regulations and rulings may subsequently affect the validity of certain sections. This information is provided to aid comprehension of state Notary Public requirements and should not be construed as legal advice. Please consult an attorney for inquiries relating to legal matters.

Sixth Edition © 2012
First Edition © 1997

ISBN: 978-1-59767-103-3

Table of Contents

For the latest updates on state laws
and requirements, please visit

NationalNotary.org/Primer-Updates

Have a Tough Notary Question?

If you were an NNA member, you could get the answer to that difficult question. Join the NNA and your membership includes access to the Notary Hotline* and live Notary experts providing the latest Notary information regarding laws, rules and regulations.

Hotline

Hours

Monday – Friday	5:00 a.m. – 7:00 p.m. (PST)
Saturdays	5:00 a.m. – 5:00 p.m. (PST)

Hotline Toll-Free Phone Number: 1-888-876-0827

After hours you can leave a message or email our experts at Hotline@NationalNotary.org and they will respond the next business day.

*Access to the Notary Hotline is for NNA members only. Call and become a member today.

Introduction

You are to be commended on your interest in Michigan Notary law! Purchasing *The Michigan Notary Law Primer* identifies you as a conscientious professional who takes your official responsibilities seriously.

In few fields is the expression "more to it than meets the eye" truer than in Notary law. What often appears on the surface to be a simple procedure may, in fact, have important legal considerations.

The purpose of *The Michigan Notary Law Primer* is to provide you with a resource to help decipher the many intricate laws that affect notarization. In doing so, the *Primer* will acquaint you with all important aspects of Michigan's Notary law and with prudent notarial practices in general.

This sixth edition of *The Michigan Notary Law Primer* includes new laws and penalties effective January 1, 2012 regarding the transfer of real property in Michigan.

While *The Michigan Notary Law Primer* begins with informative chapters on how to obtain your commission, what tools the Notary needs, often-asked questions and critical steps in notarization, the heart of this book is the chapter entitled "Notary Laws Explained." Here, we take you through the myriad of Notary laws and put them in easy-to-understand terms. Every section of the law is analyzed and explained, as well as topics not covered by Michigan law but nonetheless of vital concern to you as a Notary.

For handy reference, we have reprinted the complete text of the laws of Michigan that relate to Notaries Public. In addition, we have included addresses and phone numbers of the Department of State, county clerks' offices and Bureaus of Vital Statistics, as well as a list of nations that are parties to the Hague Convention treaty simplifying the process of authentication.

Whether you're about to be commissioned for the first time or a longtime Notary, we're sure *The Michigan Notary Law Primer* will provide you with new insight and understanding. Your improved comprehension of Michigan's Notary law will naturally result in your greater competence as a professional Notary Public.

Milton G. Valera
Chairman
National Notary Association

How to Become a Michigan Notary Public

1. Ensure that you comply with the basic qualifications for a Michigan Notary commission.

You must meet the basic requirements to become a Notary in the state of Michigan. First, you must be 18 years of age or older. Second, you must be a Michigan resident or maintain a place of business in Michigan. Third, you must reside — or, in the case of nonresidents, work — in the county in which you are requesting a commission. Fourth, you must be able to read and write English. And fifth, you must be free of felony or misdemeanor convictions (within the past 10 years) or other disqualifying violations listed in the Michigan Compiled Laws 55.301 — see page 81. A prisoner or inmate is not eligible.

U.S. citizenship is not required to become a Michigan Notary, though any noncitizen applicant should be a legally-residing resident. As a result of a 1984 U.S. Supreme Court decision, *Bernal v. Fainter*, no person may be denied a Notary commission merely on the basis of lack of U.S. citizenship.

2. Obtain a commission application and Notary information materials.

Notary applicants may obtain a commission application from the Department of State or a county clerk. Applicants should also request a copy of the applicable Michigan statutes relating to Notaries Public, reprinted in this *Primer* starting on page 70. To have an application form and information materials mailed to you, contact the Department of State at (517) 373-2531.

Should you choose to receive the application from the county clerk, a list of county clerk offices is provided on pages 94–98.

For current Notaries seeking to renew their commissions, there is no special reappointment process. Second and subsequent commissions will be issued as if for the first time. To avoid a lapse in notarial powers, applications for another term may be submitted in advance, but no earlier than 60 days before the expiration of the current commission.

3. Study the applicable Michigan statutes.

Along with the commission application, you should also obtain a copy of the applicable Michigan statutes. Although Michigan does not require prospective Notaries to pass an exam, the statutes should be studied thoroughly to become familiar with notarial acts and duties.

It is also helpful to review the "Notary Laws Explained" chapter of this *Primer,* starting on page 19. The pertinent Michigan Notary statutes are reprinted in the back of this *Primer*, beginning on page 70.

4. File your oath and bond.

Within 90 days before filing an application for a Notary commission, the applicant must file a $10,000 surety bond and take the oath of office with the clerk of the county of residence or employment. The $10,000 surety bond must be obtained from a surety company licensed to do business in the state. The fee for filing the bond and oath in most counties is $10.

Upon filing the oath and bond, the applicant will be given a certificate of filing to be submitted with the application. Effective April 1, 2007, an attorney licensed by the State Bar of Michigan applying for a Notary commission is no longer required to post the required $10,000 bond (MCL 55.271[f]).

5. Complete the application.

Follow the clear instructions on the application and complete the form in blue or black ink. On the application, you may not use a post office box as an address. In addition, a married woman must use her own name, not that of her spouse (for example, "Jane Smith," not "Mrs. John Smith"). Sign and date the form.

Be aware that any incorrect or omitted information required by this form may be cause for the Department of State to return the application to the would-be Notary until the information is correct and complete. In addition to other information that may be required by the Secretary, the application shall include all of the following:

- Applicant's name, residence address, business address, date of birth and residence and business telephone numbers.
- Applicant's driver's license or state identification card number.
- Copy of the bond and oath certificate of filing.
- If applicable, a statement showing whether the applicant has previously applied for a Notary commission in Michigan or another state, the result of the application and whether the applicant ever had a Notary commission revoked in Michigan or another state.
- Statement describing any felony or other conviction for the 10 years prior to the application.
- Declaration that the applicant is a citizen of the United States or proof of the applicant's legal residence in the U.S.
- Applicant's affirmation that the application is correct, that the applicant has read the Notary statutes and that the applicant will perform faithfully as a Notary.

Mail the completed and endorsed form with a check or money order in the amount of $10 (payable to the "State of Michigan") to: Michigan Department of State, Office of the Great Seal, 7064 Crowner Drive, Lansing, MI 48918.

If the fee check accompanying the application is returned for insufficient funds, the commission is automatically canceled. (See page 20.)

6. Wait for notice of appointment by the state.

After approval of the application, the Secretary will mail the certificate of appointment directly to the applicant. The certificate of appointment will identify the person as a Notary Public and will specify the term of the person's commission.

If rejected, the applicant will receive the application with a rejection notice asking for correction and resubmission.

To inquire as to the status of a Notary application, contact the Department of State at (888) SOS-MICH. ■

Tools of the Trade

Notaries need several important tools in order to carry out their duties lawfully and efficiently. These tools are as important to the Notary as a hammer and saw are to the carpenter.

Inking Seal

The inking seal is the Notary's official seal. Although seal use is not required by Michigan law, many of the state's Notaries elect to use an inking stamp to impart an appropriate sense of ceremony to their official acts. There is a very practical reason for using a Notary seal on notarized documents sent to other states and foreign nations: the absence of a seal may delay or, on occasion in foreign nations, even prevent the document's acceptance.

Further, an inking seal allows the Notary to comply with the Michigan statute requiring that the following be affixed in a photographically reproducible manner near the Notary's signature on every document notarized:

1) The Notary's name as it appears on the commission application.

2) The words, "Notary Public, State of Michigan, County of __________," with the county of commissioning filled in the blank.

3) The completed statement, "My commission expires ________."

4) If notarizing in a county other than the county of commissioning, the words, "Acting in the county of ________," with the blank filled in properly (MCL 55.289).

Although the "Michigan Notary Public Act" states that a Notary may use "a stamp seal or electronic process," there are no approved procedures in place for electronic notarization (Public Act 238 of '03, Sect. 27[3]).

Seal Embosser

While not required by Michigan law, the seal embosser is used in many states and is often vital on documents sent abroad. Some Michigan Notaries opt to affix an embossment in addition to an inking seal impression. The seal embosser makes a nonphotographically reproducible indentation on the document. Because photocopies of documents can easily pass as originals, the embossment can be used to distinguish an original from a photocopy. Also, embossing all pages in a document together can safeguard against later fraudulent replacement of pages.

Journal of Notarial Acts

Though Michigan law does not directly address the use of journals, the National Notary Association and state officials recommend that all Notaries maintain a complete and accurate record of all notarial acts.

Keeping a journal is a businesslike practice that demonstrates the Notary's professional care. The Notary's journal provides a record that may be used as evidence in a court proceeding, and it may protect the Notary against claims of misconduct or negligence.

Information recorded in the journal should include the date, time and type of each official act; the document date; the type of document notarized; the signature and printed name and address of each person whose signature is notarized; the type of information used to verify the identity of the signers; the fee charged; and any additional comments the Notary considers important.

Bound Notary journals with numbered pages have proved to be the safest and most fraud-resistant type of record book. By contrast, loose-leaf books are the least secure.

Jurat Stamp

The jurat stamp impresses on an affidavit the jurat wording, "Subscribed and sworn to before me this ____________ day of _______, _____ by ____________." More convenient (and safer, since critical wording will not be omitted) than typing the wording on each affidavit that requires it, the jurat stamp is both handy and practical.

Venue Stamp

The venue stamp is used in conjunction with the jurat stamp in a jurat. The phrase, "State of ____________, County of ____________," indicates where the jurat was executed. This stamp can also be used for acknowledgments and other notarial acts.

Fingerprinting Device

Increasingly, Notaries are requiring signers to affix a thumbprint in the journal. A fingerprint serves as proof that a signer did or did not appear, thereby deterring forgers. Many Notaries opt for the convenience of an inexpensive device that allows one finger at a time to be printed.

Notarial Certificates

Notarial certificates for acknowledgments, jurats ("verifications upon oath or affirmation"), proofs of execution by subscribing witness and for copy certifications by a document custodian are available.

Errors and Omissions Insurance

Notary errors and omissions insurance provides protection for Notaries who are sued for damages resulting from unintentional notarial mistakes. In the event of a lawsuit, the "E&O" insurance company will provide and pay for the Notary's legal counsel and absorb any damages levied by a court or agreed to in a settlement, up to the policy coverage limit. Errors and omissions insurance does not cover the Notary for intentional or negligent misconduct. ■

As a full-service organization, the National Notary Association makes available to Michigan Notaries all notarial items required by law, custom and convenience.

10 Most-Asked Questions

Every Notary has a question or two about whether and how to notarize. But there are certain questions that pop up again and again. These top 10 are asked repeatedly at the National Notary Association's seminars, its annual National Conference of Notaries Public and through its *Notary Information Service*.

As with most questions about notarization, the answer to these 10 is not always a simple "yes" or "no." Rather, the answer is, "It depends ..."

Here's what every Notary wants to know:

1. Can I notarize a will?

Laws regarding wills differ from state to state. Some states do not require notarization of wills, while others allow it as one of several witnessing options. Usually, it is not the will itself that is notarized, but accompanying affidavits signed by witnesses.

A Notary should only notarize a will if clear instructions and a notarial certificate are provided. If the signer of the will is relying on the Notary for advice on how to proceed, the Notary should ask the individual to find an attorney.

The danger in notarizing wills is that would-be testators who have drafted their own wills without legal advice may believe that notarization will make their wills legal and valid. However, even when notarized, such homemade wills may be worthless because the testators failed to obtain the proper number of witnesses or omitted important information.

In fact, notarization itself may actually void an otherwise properly executed handwritten (holographic) will, because courts have occasionally held that any writing on the document other than the testator's invalidates the will.

2. Can I notarize for a stranger who does not have identification?

Yes. If identification of a signer cannot be based on personal knowledge or identification documents (ID cards), a Notary may rely on the oath or affirmation of a personally known credible identifying witness to identify an unknown signer.

If a credible identifying witness is used, the Notary must personally know the credible identifying witness, who, in turn, must personally know the document signer. This establishes a "chain of personal knowledge" from the Notary to the credible identifying witness to the signer.

A credible identifying witness should be someone the Notary believes to be trustworthy and impartial. If a person has a financial or other beneficial interest in a document, or is named in the document, that individual could not be a reliable witness.

When no credible identifying witness is available to identify the signer and the signer is unable to obtain an adequate identification document, the Notary may have no choice but to tell the signer to find a personally known Notary or a friend who personally knows a Notary.

3. Can I notarize a photograph?

No. To simply stamp and sign a photograph is improper. A Notary's signature and seal must appear only on a notarial certificate (such as an acknowledgment or jurat) accompanying a written statement signed by another person.

However, a signature on a written statement referring to an accompanying or attached photograph may be notarized; if the photograph is large enough, the statement and notarial certificate might even appear on its reverse side. Such a format may be acceptable when notarized photos are requested by persons seeking medical or health licenses, or by legal resident aliens renewing foreign passports.

A word of caution here: a Notary should always be suspicious about notarizing a photo-bearing card or document that could be used as a bogus "official" ID.

4. What if there's no room to affix my seal or stamp required wording or if either smears?

Usually, if notarial wording printed on a document leaves no room for a seal or required wording, a so-called loose certificate can be attached and filled out instead, if the attached certificate wording is substantially the same as on the document.

If an initial seal impression is illegible and there is ample room on the document, another impression can be affixed nearby. The illegibility of the first impression will indicate why a second seal impression was necessary. And the Notary should record in the journal that a second seal was applied.

A Notary should never attempt to fix an imperfect seal impression with pen, ink or correction fluid. This may be viewed as evidence of tampering and cause the document's rejection by a recorder.

5. Can I notarize signatures on photocopies of documents?

Yes. A photocopy may be notarized as long as it bears an original signature. That is, the photocopy must have been signed with pen and ink. A photocopied signature itself may never be notarized.

However, some public recorders will not accept notarized signatures on photocopied sheets because they will not adequately reproduce in microfilming.

When carbon copies of notarized documents are made, the Notary will sometimes be asked to conform rather than to notarize the copies. To conform a copy, the Notary reaffixes the official seal on the copy (carbon will not readily transfer a seal impression), prints out any notarial wording that may not have transferred and writes "Conformed Copy" prominently across the top of the copy. Conforming a copy is not a notarial act.

6. Can I notarize for customers only?

As a public official, a Notary is not commissioned to serve just the customers or clients of any one business, even when the employer has paid for the bond, commissioning fees and notarial supplies. There is no such officer as a "Notary Private."

Discrimination against anyone who presents a lawful request for notarization can be problematic for a public official commissioned to serve all of the public equally. Such discrimination can provide the basis for lawsuits.

Yet, Michigan allows a Notary and employer to agree to limit the Notary's services to transactions directly related to the employer's business during business hours.

7. Can I notarize a document in a language I can't read?

Yes. As long as the notarial certificate and document signature are in a language the Notary can read, Michigan Notaries are not expressly prohibited from notarizing documents written in languages they cannot read.

However, there are certain difficulties and dangers in notarizing documents that the Notary cannot read. The main difficulty for the Notary is making an accurate journal description of an unreadable document; the main danger is that the document may be blatantly fraudulent.

Under no circumstances should a notarization be performed if the Notary and the principal signer cannot communicate in the same language.

8. Can I certify a copy of a birth certificate?

No. Some states — although not Michigan — do allow Notaries to certify copies, but copies of documents that are either public records or publicly recordable should never be certified by any Notaries. Only an officer in a bureau of vital statistics should ever certify a copy of a birth certificate or other vital public record; a Notary's "certification" of a birth or death record may actually lend credibility to a counterfeit or tampered document. Only a county recording official should certify a copy of a deed or other recordable instrument.

In states allowing Notary-certified copies, the types of document copies that Notaries may properly certify are original personal papers such as letters and college diplomas, and in-house business documents.

9. Does a document have to be signed in my presence?

No and yes. Documents requiring acknowledgments normally do not need to be signed in the Notary's presence. However, the signer must appear before the Notary at the time of notarization to acknowledge that he or she freely signed for the purposes stated in the document.

An acknowledgment certificate indicates that the signer personally appeared before the Notary, was identified by the Notary and acknowledged to the Notary that the document was freely signed.

On the other hand, documents requiring a jurat ("verification upon oath or affirmation") must be signed in the Notary's presence, as dictated by the typical jurat wording, "Subscribed (signed) and sworn to before me ..."

In executing a jurat, a Notary guarantees that the signer: personally appeared before the Notary, was given an oath or affirmation by the Notary and signed the document in the Notary's presence. In addition, state law requires that the Notary positively identify a signer for a jurat.

10. Can I notarize for a family member?

No. Notaries are prohibited from notarizing for a lineal ancestor. "Lineal ancestor" is defined as an individual in the direct line of ascent including, but not limited to, a parent or grandparent.

Besides the possibility of a financial interest in notarizing for a relative, there may be an "emotional interest" that can prevent the Notary from acting impartially. For example, a Notary who is asked to notarize a contract signed by his father might attempt to persuade the parent to sign or not sign. As a close family member, the individual is entitled to exert influence — but this is entirely improper for a Notary.

Even if a Notary has no direct beneficial interest in the document and does not attempt to influence the signer, notarizing for a relative could subject the document to a legal challenge if others affected by the transaction allege that the Notary could not have acted impartially. ■

Steps to Proper Notarization

What constitutes reasonable care?

If a Notary can convincingly show that he or she used every reasonable precaution expected of a person of ordinary prudence and intelligence, then the Notary has exercised reasonable care — a shield against liability.

The following 14-step checklist will help Notaries apply the principles associated with reasonable care and avert the most common pitfalls.

1. Require every signer to personally appear.

The signer must appear in person before the Notary on the date and in the county stated in the venue on the notarial certificate. "Personal appearance" means the signer is in the Notary's physical presence — face to face in the same room. A telephone call is not acceptable as personal appearance.

2. Make a careful identification.

The Notary should identify every document signer through either personal knowledge, the word of a personally known credible identifying witness under oath or through reliable identification documents (ID cards).

When using ID cards, the Notary must examine them closely to detect alteration, counterfeiting or evidence that they were issued to an impostor. Don't rely on a type of card with which you are unfamiliar, unless you check it against a reference such as the *U.S. Identification Manual* or the *ID Checking Guide*.

3. Feel certain the signer is aware.

A conscientious and careful Notary will be certain not only of the signer's identity and willingness to sign, but will also make a layperson's judgment about the signer's ability to understand the document. This ability to understand is called competence.

A document signer who cannot respond intelligibly in a simple conversation with the Notary should not be considered competent to sign at that moment. If in doubt, the Notary can ask the signer if he or she understands the document and can explain its purpose. Or, if in a medical environment, the signer's doctor can be consulted for a professional opinion.

4. Check the signature.

The Notary must make sure that the document signer signs the same, or an abbreviated version, name appearing on the identification presented.

To check for possible forgery, the Notary should compare the signature that the person leaves in the Notary's journal against the signatures on the document and on the IDs. Also, it should be noted whether the signer appears to be laboring on the journal signature, a possible indication of a forgery in progress.

In certain circumstances, it may be acceptable for a signer to sign with an abbreviated form of his or her name (John D. Smith instead of John David Smith, for example), as long as the individual is signing with less than and not more than what is on the identification document.

5. Look for blank spaces.

Documents with blank spaces have a great potential for fraudulent misuse. A borrower, for example, might sign an incomplete promissory note, trusting the lender to fill it out, and then later find that the lender has written in an amount in excess of what was actually borrowed.

If the blanks are inapplicable and intended to be left unfilled, the signer should be asked to line through each space (using ink), or to write in "Not Applicable" or "N/A."

6. Scan the document.

Notaries are not required to read the documents they notarize. However, they should note certain important particulars about a document, such as its title, for recording in the Notary's journal. Notaries must be sure to count and record the number of pages; this can show whether pages are later fraudulently added or removed.

7. Check the document's date.

For acknowledgments, the date of signing on the document must either precede or be the same as the date of the notarization but not follow it. Since a person must sign in front of a Notary for the execution of a jurat ("verification upon oath or affirmation"), the document signing date and the notarization date must be the same for that type of notarial act.

A document dated to follow the date on its notarial certificate risks rejection by a recorder, who may question how the document could have been notarized before it was signed.

8. Keep a journal of notarial acts.

Although not required by Michigan law, a journal is recommended for all Notaries. If a notarized document is lost or altered, or if certain facts about the transaction are later challenged, the Notary's journal becomes valuable evidence. It can protect the rights of all parties to a transaction and help Notaries defend themselves against false accusations.

The Notary should include all the pertinent details of the notarization in the journal, such as the date, time and type of notarization; the date, type and number of pages of the document; the signature, printed name and address of the signer; how the person was identified; and notarial fees charged, if any. Any other pertinent data, such as observations made by the Notary about the signer's awareness or a capacity claimed by the signer, may also be entered.

9. Complete the journal entry first.

The Notary should complete the journal entry entirely before filling out the notarial certificate. This prevents a signer from leaving before the important public record of the notarization is made in the journal.

10. Make sure the document has notarial wording.

If a notarial certificate does not come with the document, the Notary must ask the document signer what type of notarization — acknowledgment or jurat — is required. The Notary may then type the appropriate notarial wording on the document or attach a "loose" certificate.

If the signer does not know what type of notarization is required, he or she should contact the document's issuing or receiving agency to determine this. This decision is never the Notary's to make unless the Notary is also an attorney.

11. Be attentive to details.

When filling out the certificate, the Notary needs to make sure that the venue correctly identifies the place of notarization; if the venue is preprinted and incorrect, the Notary must line through the incorrect state and/or county, write in the proper site of the notarization and initial and date the change.

Also, the Notary must pay attention to spaces on the notarial certificate that indicate the number and gender of the document signers, as well as how they were identified — for example, leave the plural "(s)" untouched or cross it out, as appropriate.

12. Affix signature (and seal) properly.

Notaries should sign exactly the same name that appears on their commission application. The seal, if used, should be placed as close to the Notary's signature as possible without overprinting it. To prevent illegibility, a Notary seal should not be affixed over wording, particularly over a signature. Although an embossment may be placed over the letters "L.S.," an inked seal should be affixed next to but not over the letters to ensure legibility of the data in the seal. Michigan and several other states do not require Notaries to use seals. However, Michigan Notaries are required to print, type, stamp or otherwise imprint mechanically or electronically on the notarial certificate in a photographically reproducible manner their name and title ("Notary Public"); the name of the state and county in which they are commissioned; the commission expiration date; the date the notarial act was performed; and, if notarizing in a county other than the county of commissioning, the statement, "Acting in the County of ________."

13. Protect 'loose' certificates.

If the Notary has to attach a notarial certificate, it should be securely stapled to the left margin of the document. Notaries can protect against the removal of such a loose certificate by embossing it together with the document and writing the particulars of the document to which the certificate is attached on the certificate. For example, the notation, "This certificate is attached to a 15-page partnership agreement between John Smith and Mary Doe, signed July 14, 2010," would deter fraudulent removal and reattachment of a loose certificate.

14. Don't give advice.

Every state prohibits nonattorneys from practicing law. Notaries should never prepare or complete documents for others, or give advice on any matter relating to a document unless they are attorneys or professionals certified or licensed in a relevant area of expertise. The nonattorney Notary never chooses the type of certificate or notarization a document requires, since this decision can have important legal ramifications. The Notary could be held liable for any damages resulting from an incorrectly chosen certificate or notarization. ■

Notary Laws Explained

In layperson's language, this chapter discusses and clarifies pertinent sections of the Michigan Compiled Laws (MCL) that regulate Notaries Public. The statutes are reprinted in full in "Michigan Laws Pertaining to Notaries Public," beginning on page 71.

THE NOTARY COMMISSION

Application for New Commission

Qualifications. To become a first-time Notary in Michigan, or to renew a commission, the applicant (MCL 55.271[1]):

1) Must be at least 18 years old.

2) Must be a resident of Michigan and a resident of the county in which the applicant seeks an appointment or a nonresident who maintains a principal place of business in Michigan.

3) Must be able to read, write and speak the English language.

4) Must be free of felony or misdemeanor convictions (within the past 10 years) or other disqualifying violations listed in the Michigan Notary Public Act, Section 41.

Citizenship. U.S. citizenship is not required to become a Michigan Notary, though any noncitizen applicant should be a legally residing alien. A 1984 Supreme Court decision, *Bernal v. Fainter*, declared that no state may deny a Notary commission merely on the basis of lack of U.S. citizenship.

Incomplete Application. The Department of State may reject an application if it is incomplete. The application will be returned to the applicant and will require resubmission.

Application Fee. A nonrefundable application fee of $10 must be submitted with the application. An additional fee will be required at the time of filing the official oath of office and bond with the county clerk (MCL 55.275[g][2]).

The Secretary shall automatically cancel the Notary Public commission of any person who makes, draws, utters or delivers any check, draft or order of payment of a processing fee that is not honored by the bank, financial institution or other depository expected to render payment upon its first presentation (MCL 55.279[4]).

Nonresident Applicants. In addition to the application requirements for residents, nonresident applicants must indicate that they maintain a principal place of business in the county where they are requesting appointment. Such applicants must also demonstrate that their business activity will require them to perform notarial acts (MCL 55.271[e]).

Notification of Appointment

Notification by Secretary of State. After approval of the application, the Secretary of State will mail the certificate of appointment as a Notary Public directly to the applicant. The certificate of appointment will identify the person as a Notary Public of the State of Michigan and will specify the term of the new Notary's commission.

Application for Reappointment

Reappointment. A Notary's term lasts for six to seven years, ending on the Notary's birthday, not less than six or more than seven years from the date of appointment. A Notary seeking reappointment must apply for a new commission and follow the same procedures as when applying for a commission for the first time (MCL 55.279[2]).

To avoid a lapse in notarial powers, a Notary may submit an application for another term in advance, but no earlier than 60 days prior to expiration of the current appointment.

Attorneys. Licensed attorneys are not granted automatic notarial powers. An attorney must apply for a commission.

Reappointment for Attorneys

1) The Secretary of State must send a reappointment application form to a licensed attorney granted an appointment as a Notary at least 90 days before the expiration of the current appointment.

2) The application for reappointment must contain a certification to be completed by the applicant certifying that he or she was still a member in good standing of the State Bar of Michigan (MCL 55.279[3]).

Exam

Not Required. An exam is not required to obtain a first or subsequent Notary commission.

Notary Bond

Requirement. Michigan Notaries are required to obtain a $10,000 bond and file it at the office of the clerk in the county where the Notary has been appointed (MCL 55.273[1]).

Filing the Bond. Within 90 calendar days prior to submitting an application for appointment as a Notary Public, the applicant must file a $10,000 bond with the county clerk of the county of residence (or in the case of out-of-state applicants, the county of employment) and take the oath prescribed by the Constitution. The commission will not be issued to the applicant until the oath and bond have been filed (MCL 55.273[1]).

Surety. The surety for the Notary's bond must be a company licensed to issue bonds in the state (MCL 55.273[2]).

Not Required for Attorneys. An attorney licensed by the State Bar of Michigan applying for a Notary commission is no longer required to post the required $10,000 bond (MCL 55.271[f]).

Protects Public. The Notary surety bond protects the public from a Notary's misconduct or negligence; it does *not* protect the Notary. Up to the coverage limit, the bond provides reimbursement for damages to anyone who suffers financially due to an improper official act on the part of the Notary. The surety will seek compensation from the Notary for any damages it has to pay out on the Notary's behalf.

Liable for All Damages. Both the Notary and surety company may be sued for damages resulting from notarial misconduct. The surety is liable only up to the amount of the bond, but the Notary may be found liable for any amount of money for damages deemed to have been caused by the Notary's improper acts.

Liability. As ministerial officials, Notaries generally may be held financially responsible for any and all damages caused by their mistakes or misconduct in performing notarial acts.

If a person is financially injured by a Notary's negligence or willful failure to properly perform a notarial act — whether intentional or unintentional — the Notary may be sued in civil court and ordered to pay all resulting damages, including attorneys' fees (MCL 55.273[2]).

A person need not be named in a document to sue a Notary for damages resulting from the Notary's handling of that document. If, for example, a lender accepts a forged, notarized deed as collateral for a loan, the lender might sue to recover losses from the Notary who witnessed the bogus deed.

Errors and Omissions Insurance. Up to the policy coverage limit, errors and omissions insurance will absorb a Notary's expenses in defending against a lawsuit caused by that Notary's honest and unintentional mistake.

Oath of Office

Requirement. Within 90 days before submitting an application for a Notary Public appointment, Michigan Notaries are required to take and file an oath of office (MCL 55.273[1]).

Filing the Oath. The oath must be taken and filed within 90 days prior to submitting the application for commission.

To take the oath, the applicant must appear before the county clerk of the county in which the Notary seeks to be appointed. The clerk will administer the required oath, in which the applicant swears to faithfully and honestly discharge the duties of the office of Notary Public for Michigan (MCL 55.273[3]).

Fee. The county clerk will charge at least a $10 fee to file and record the Notary's oath (MCL 55.273[3]). After the fee is paid, the county clerk will give a bond and oath certificate to the applicant.

A county with a population of more than two million may impose a fee different from the amount cited above.

Jurisdiction

Statewide. Michigan Notaries may perform official acts throughout the state of Michigan but not beyond the state borders. They are not limited to just the respective counties in which they live (MCL 55.269[2]).

However, a Notary must reside in the county in which he or she has been appointed. If notarization takes place in a county other than the county in which the Notary is appointed, the Notary must add the completed words "Acting in the County of ________" to the certificate (MCL 55.287[2]).

The Notary may not witness a signing outside of Michigan and then return to the state to perform the notarization. All parts of a given notarization must be performed at the same time and place within the state of Michigan.

Michigan Notaries may notarize documents originating in another state or nation, as long as the requested notarial act complies with Michigan law. In such cases, they should ensure that the venue — the place of notarization — is correctly written on the certificate.

Term of Office

Six-to Seven-Year Term. The term of office for a Michigan Notary Public is six to seven years, depending on the Notary's birthday. Each term begins with the date specified by the Department of State and ends on the Notary's birthday, not less than six years or more than seven years after the appointment, unless the appointment is officially canceled, suspended or revoked by the state (MCL 55.269[2]).

Resignation

Notification. To resign, the National Notary Association recommends that a Notary submit a written notice to the Department of State, giving an effective date. Such a resignation is appropriate if the Notary moves out of the state. The notice should be sent by certified mail.

A copy of the resignation notice may also be sent to the office of the county clerk where the Notary has filed the oath and bond.

Disposition of Seal and Records. If the resigning Notary has a seal of office or a stamp that he or she used to affix information on certificates, these should be destroyed or defaced to prevent fraudulent use. If the Notary maintained a journal of notarial acts or other recordbook, the National Notary Association recommends that the Notary retain and safeguard the records until passage of the pertinent statute of limitations.

Death of Notary

Notification. If a Notary should die, the Notary's personal representative should notify the Department of State. The notification should include the Notary's name and appointment number, as well as any additional pertinent information, and should be sent by certified mail.

Disposition of Seal and Records. If the deceased Notary used a seal or stamp to affix information on notarial certificates, these should be destroyed or defaced to prevent fraudulent use. If the Notary maintained a journal or other recordbook, the National Notary Association recommends that the Notary's personal representative retain the journal in keeping with the pertinent statute of limitations.

Change of Address

Notification Required. If there is a change in the Notary's residence or business address, the Notary must immediately apply to the Secretary of State for a corrected Notary commission (MCL 55.281[1]).

Change of Name

Notification. When a Notary changes name, he or she must immediately apply to the Secretary of State for a corrected Notary commission (MCL 55.281[1]).

OFFICIAL NOTARIAL ACTS

Authorized Acts

Notaries may perform the following official acts:

- Acknowledgments, certifying that a signer personally appeared before the Notary, was identified by the Notary and acknowledged freely signing the document (MCL 55.263[a] and 55.285[2]). (See pages 26–29.)

- Verifications upon oath or affirmation (jurats), as found in affidavits and other sworn documents, certifying that the signer personally appeared before the Notary, was identified by the Notary, signed in the Notary's presence and took an oath or affirmation from the Notary (MCL 55.265[a], 55.267[d] and 55.285[3]). (See pages 33–34.)

- Oaths and affirmations, which are solemn promises to God (oath) or solemn promises on one's own personal honor (affirmation) (MCL 55.285[1b]). (See pages 34–35.)

- Proofs of Execution, certifying that a subscribing witness personally appeared and swore to the Notary that another person, the principal, signed a document (MCL 565.262). (See pages 35–37.)

- Witnessings or attestations of signatures, certifying that the signer personally appeared before the Notary, was identified and signed in the Notary's presence (MCL 55.285[4]). (See pages 37–38.)

Unauthorized Acts

Certified Copies of Public Records. A certified copy is a duplicate of an original document that is certified as an exact reproduction. In Michigan, a Notary is prohibited from issuing certified copies of public records or any other documents.

Requests for certified copies should be directed to the agency that holds or issued the original. For example, a certified copy of a birth certificate can be obtained from the Bureau of Vital Statistics (or the equivalent) in the state where the person was born.

An alternative to a Notary-certified copy is copy certification by document custodian. Here the permanent keeper of a document — the custodian — certifies the duplicate in a written statement, and the Notary executes a jurat for the custodian's signature. (See "Copy Certification by Document Custodian," pages 29–31.)

Marriages. Michigan Notaries have no authority to perform marriages unless they are also ministers. Only Notaries in Maine, South Carolina and Florida are empowered to perform marriages strictly by virtue of holding a notarial commission. (See "Weddings," page 60.)

Notary's Own Signature. Notaries are never permitted to notarize their own signatures (MCL 55.291[2][a]).

Telephone Notarizations. State law requires that a document signer must personally appear before the Notary, face to face in the same room, at the time of the notarization, not before, not after. Acknowledgments and jurats may not be performed over the telephone (MCL 565.264 and 565.266).

Wills. Notaries may not draft wills nor offer advice concerning a will. A Notary should only notarize a document described as a will if a notarial certificate is provided or stipulated and the would-be testator is not asking questions about how to proceed. Any such questions should be answered only by an attorney. (See "Wills," pages 59–60.)

Acknowledgments

A Common Notarial Act. Acknowledgments are one of the most common forms of notarization. Typically, they are executed on deeds and other documents that will be publicly recorded by a county official.

Purpose. In executing an acknowledgment, a Notary certifies three things (MCL 565.264):

1) The signer personally appeared before the Notary on the date and in the county indicated on the notarial certificate (notarization cannot be based on a telephone call or on a Notary's familiarity with a signature).

2) The signer was positively identified by the Notary through either personal knowledge or satisfactory evidence. (See "Identifying Document Signers," pages 38–42).

3) The signer acknowledged to the Notary that the signature was freely made for the purposes stated in the document. (If a document is willingly signed in the presence of the Notary, this tacit act can serve just as well as an oral statement of acknowledgment.)

Certificates for Acknowledgment. Upon taking the acknowledgment of any document signer, the Notary must complete, sign and seal (if used) an appropriate certificate of acknowledgment. The certificate wording should either be preprinted or typed at the end of the document, or appear as an attachment (a "loose" certificate) that is stapled to the document's signature page.

Michigan law provides "statutory short forms of acknowledgment" which may be used and are sufficient for their purposes under any law of the state. Use of other appropriate forms is not prohibited (MCL 565.267).

- Acknowledgment for an individual acting in his or her own behalf:

State of Michigan
County of ____________

The foregoing instrument was acknowledged before me this ___________ (date) by ___________ (name of person acknowledging).

____________ (Signature of Notary) (Stamp of Notary)

(If not in stamp, print or type Notary's name; "Notary Public, State of Michigan, County of _______;" "My commission expires _______;" if acting in another county other than the county of commissioning, "Acting in the County of _______;" and the date the notarial act was performed.)

- Acknowledgment for a corporation:

State of Michigan
County of ____________

The foregoing instrument was acknowledged before me this ___________ (date) by ___________ (name of officer or agent, title of officer or agent) of ___________ (name of corporation acknowledging), a ___________ (state or place of incorporation) corporation, on behalf of the corporation.

____________ (Signature of Notary) (Stamp of Notary)

(If not in stamp, print or type Notary's name; "Notary Public, State of Michigan, County of _______;" "My commission expires _______;" if acting in another county other than the county of commissioning, "Acting in the County of _______;" and the date the notarial act was performed.)

- Acknowledgment for a partnership:

State of Michigan
County of ____________

The foregoing instrument was acknowledged before me this ___________ (date) by ___________ (name of acknowledging partner or agent), partner (or agent) on behalf of ___________ (name of partnership), a partnership.

____________ (Signature of Notary) (Stamp of Notary)

(If not in stamp, print or type Notary's name; "Notary Public, State of Michigan, County of _______;" "My commission expires _______;" if acting in another county other than the county of commissioning, "Acting in the County of _______;" and the date the notarial act was performed.)

- Acknowledgment for an attorney in fact on behalf of an absent principal:

State of Michigan
County of ___________

The foregoing instrument was acknowledged before me this ___________ (date) by ___________ (name of attorney in fact) as attorney in fact on behalf of ___________ (name of principal).
___________ (Signature of Notary) (Stamp of Notary)

(If not in stamp, print or type Notary's name; "Notary Public, State of Michigan, County of ________;" "My commission expires ________;" if acting in another county other than the county of commissioning, "Acting in the County of ________;" and the date the notarial act was performed.)

- Acknowledgment for a public officer, trustee or personal representative:

State of Michigan
County of ___________

The foregoing instrument was acknowledged before me this ___________ (date) by ___________ (name and title of position).

___________ (Signature of Notary) (Stamp of Notary)

(If not in stamp, print or type Notary's name; "Notary Public, State of Michigan, County of ________;" "My commission expires ________;" if acting in another county other than the county of commissioning, "Acting in the County of ________"; and the date the notarial act was performed.)

Alternate Acknowledgment Certificate. Other forms of acknowledgment certificates are acceptable if (MCL 565.265):

- The certificate is in a form prescribed by the laws or regulations of the state of Michigan.

- The certificate is in a form applicable to the place in which the acknowledgment is taken.

- The certificate contains the words "acknowledged before me" or substantially similar wording.

Required Information. Although Michigan law does not require the use of an inking seal or embosser, the following information must be typed, printed, stamped or otherwise imprinted mechanically or electronically in a photographically reproducible manner on each notarial certificate (MCL 55.287[2]):

- The Notary's name as it appears on the commission application.
- "Notary Public, State of Michigan, County of __________."
- "My commission expires__________."
- If notarizing in a county other than the county of commissioning, the statement "Acting in the County of __________."
- The date the notarial act was performed.

Identification of Acknowledger. In executing an acknowledgment, the Notary must identify the signer through personal knowledge or another form of satisfactory evidence. (See "Identifying Document Signers," pages 38–42.)

Witnessing Signature. Although Michigan state officials suggest that a document requiring an acknowledgment be signed in the Notary's presence, Michigan law stipulates that a signer must appear before the Notary at the time of notarization to acknowledge having signed the document (MCL 565.264).

In most states, a document could be signed an hour before, a week before, a year before, etc. — as long as the signer appears before the Notary with the signed document at the time of notarization to admit that the signature is his or her own. (However, for a jurat notarization, which requires an oath or affirmation, the document must indeed be signed in the presence of the Notary. See "Jurats," pages 33–34.)

Terminology. In discussing acknowledgments, it is important to use proper terminology. A Notary takes or executes an acknowledgment, while a document signer makes or gives an acknowledgment.

Fees. A Notary may charge up to $10 for taking an acknowledgment (MCL 55.285[7]).

Copy Certification by Document Custodian

Purpose. While not an official notarial act, copy certification by document custodian may serve as an alternative to a Notary-certified document copy in jurisdictions, such as Michigan, where it is unlawful for an original document to be copied or certified by a Notary.

It should be noted that copy certification by document custodian may not always be an acceptable substitute for a Notary-certified copy, so the person requesting the act should check to be sure that it will serve the required purposes.

Procedure. The permanent keeper of the document, the document custodian, not the Notary, certifies the copy. The custodian makes a photocopy of the original document; makes a written statement about the trueness, correctness and completeness of the copy; signs that statement before a Notary; and takes an oath or affirmation regarding the truth of the statement. The Notary, having witnessed the signing and given the oath or affirmation, executes a jurat.

Not for Vital Records. Copy certification by document custodian is not appropriate for vital records — such as birth, marriage and death certificates — unless the certificate is signed by the public custodian in charge of the vital records. Persons requesting certified copies of vital records should be directed to the agency that holds the original — typically, the Bureau of Vital Statistics or county clerk in the area where the birth, death or marriage occurred.

Certificate for Copy Certification by Document Custodian. In addition to the jurat certificate, a statement by the custodian — attesting to the truth and accuracy of the document — is required. Although not prescribed by law, this wording is recommended by the National Notary Association:

> I, ___________ (name of custodian of original document), hereby swear (or affirm) that the attached reproduction of ___________ (description of original document) is a true, correct and complete photocopy of a document in my possession.
>
> ___________ (signature of custodian) ___________ (address)
>
> State of Michigan
> County of ___________
>
> Subscribed and sworn to (or affirmed) before me this ______ day of ___________ (month), _____ (year), by ___________ (name of custodian).
>
> ____________ (Signature of Notary) (Stamp of Notary)

(If not in stamp, print or type Notary's name; "Notary Public, State of Michigan, County of ________;" "My commission expires ________;" if acting in another county other than the county of commissioning, "Acting in the County of ________;" and the date the notarial act was performed.)

Depositions and Affidavits

Purpose. A deposition is a signed transcript of the signer's oral statements taken down for use in a judicial proceeding. The deposition signer is called the deponent.

An affidavit is a signed statement made under oath or affirmation by a person called an affiant, and it may be used for a variety of purposes both in and out of court.

To notarize a deposition or an affidavit, the Notary must administer an oath or affirmation and complete some form of jurat, which the Notary signs and seals.

Depositions. With a deposition, both sides in a lawsuit or court case typically have the opportunity to cross-examine the deponent. Questions and answers are transcribed into a written statement. Used only in judicial proceedings, a deposition is then signed and sworn to before an oath-administering official.

Michigan law does not empower Notaries to take depositions — meaning, to transcribe the words spoken aloud by a deponent — but Notaries may execute jurats on depositions (MCL 55.285[3]).

The actual taking of the deposition is most often done by trained and certified shorthand reporters, also known as court reporters. While most Notaries do not have the stenographic skills necessary to transcribe a deponent's words, any Notary is competent to administer an oath (or affirmation) or to execute a jurat for a deposition.

Affidavits. Affidavits are used in and out of court for a variety of purposes, from declaring losses to an insurance company to declaring U.S. citizenship before traveling to a foreign country. An affidavit is a document containing a statement voluntarily signed and sworn to or affirmed before a Notary or other official with oath-administering powers. If used in a judicial proceeding, only one side in the case need participate in the execution of the affidavit, in contrast to the deposition.

In an affidavit, the Notary's certificate typically sandwiches the affiant's signed statement, with the venue and affiant's name at the top of the document and the jurat wording at the end. The Notary is responsible for the venue, affiant's name and any notarial text at the beginning and end of the affidavit, and the affiant is responsible for the signed statement in the middle.

The following form is acceptable for an affidavit or sworn statement (MCL 55.289[2]).

State of Michigan
County of __________

I, __________ (name of affiant) (explanation of who affiant is, followed by affiant's statement).

Signature of Affiant
Printed Name of Affiant

Signed and sworn to before me in __________ County, Michigan, on __________ (month/day), ______ (year).

Notary's Stamp__________________ Notary's Signature____________________

(If not in stamp, print or type Notary's name; "Notary Public, State of Michigan, County of ________;" "My commission expires ________;" if acting in another county other than the county of commissioning, "Acting in the County of ________;" and the date the notarial act was performed.)

Certificate for Depositions and Affidavits. Depositions and affidavits require jurat certificates in some form. (See "Jurats," pages 33–34.)

Oath (Affirmation) for Depositions and Affidavits. If no other wording is prescribed in a given instance, a Notary may use the following language in administering an oath (or affirmation) for an affidavit or deposition:

> Do you solemnly swear that the statements in this document are true to the best of your knowledge and belief, so help you God?
>
> (Do you solemnly affirm that the statements in this document are true to the best of your knowledge and belief?)

For both oath and affirmation, the affiant must respond aloud and affirmatively, with "I do" or similar words. State officials suggest that the Notary and the oath-taker raise their right hands when administering the oath or affirmation.

Fees. For a jurat on a deposition or affidavit, a Notary may charge no more than $10 per signature (MCL 55.285[7]).

Jurats

Part of Verification. In notarizing affidavits, depositions and other forms of written verification requiring an oath by the signer, the Notary normally executes a jurat.

Purpose. While the purpose of an acknowledgment is to positively identify a document signer, the purpose of a jurat, also called a verification upon oath or affirmation, is to compel truthfulness by appealing to the signer's conscience and fear of criminal penalties for perjury.

In executing a jurat, a Notary certifies that (MCL 55.265[a] and 55.285[3]):

1) The signer personally appeared before the Notary at the time of notarization on the date and in the county indicated (notarization based on a telephone call or on familiarity with a signature is not acceptable).

2) The Notary positively identified the signer.

3) The Notary watched the signature being made at the time of notarization.

4) The Notary administered an oath or affirmation to the signer.

Certificate for a Jurat. A typical jurat contains the wording, "Subscribed and sworn to (or affirmed) before me" or similar language. "Subscribed" means "signed," and "before me" means that the signer personally appeared.

When jurat wording is not prescribed in a given instance, the following wording may be used:

State of Michigan
County of ____________

Subscribed and sworn to (or affirmed) before me in __________ County, Michigan, on __________ (month/day), _____ (year), by _________ (signer).

Notary's Stamp__________________ Notary's Signature____________________

(If not in stamp, print or type Notary's name; "Notary Public, State of Michigan, County of ________;" "My commission expires ________;" if acting in another county other than the county of commissioning, "Acting in the County of ________;" and the date the notarial act was performed.)

Wording for Jurat Oath (or Affirmation). If wording is not otherwise prescribed by law, a Michigan Notary may use the following or similar words to administer an oath (or affirmation) in conjunction with a jurat:

> Do you solemnly swear that the statements in this document are true to the best of your knowledge and belief, so help you God?
>
> (Do you solemnly affirm that the statements in this document are true to the best of your knowledge and belief?)

Oath or Affirmation Must Be Administered. A Notary Public does not execute a jurat by merely asking a signer whether or not the signature on an document is in fact that of the signer. An oath or affirmation must be administered and the affixation of the signature observed by the Notary.

Fees. A Notary may not charge more than $10 per signature for executing a jurat (MCL 55.285[7]).

Oaths and Affirmations

Purpose. An oath is a solemn, spoken pledge to a Supreme Being. An affirmation is a solemn, spoken pledge on one's own personal honor, with no reference to a Supreme Being. Both are usually a promise of truthfulness or fidelity and have the same legal effect.

In taking an oath or affirmation in an official proceeding, a person may be subject to criminal penalties for perjury should he or she fail to be truthful.

An oath or affirmation can be a full-fledged notarial act in its own right, as when giving an oath of office to a public official ("swearing in" a public official), or it can be part of the process of notarizing a document (e.g., executing a jurat, or swearing in a credible identifying witness).

A person who objects to taking an oath — pledging to a Supreme Being — may instead be given an affirmation.

Wording for Oath (or Affirmation). If law does not dictate otherwise, a Michigan Notary may use the following or similar words in administering an oath (or affirmation):

- Oath (Affirmation) for affiant signing an affidavit or deponent signing a deposition:

Do you solemnly swear that the statements in this document are true to the best of your knowledge and belief, so help you God?

(Do you solemnly affirm that the statements in this document are true to the best of your knowledge and belief?)

- Oath (Affirmation) for credible identifying witness:

Do you solemnly swear that you know the signer truly is the person he/she claims to be, so help you God?

(Do you solemnly affirm that you know the signer truly is the person he/she claims to be?)

The person taking the oath or affirmation must respond by repeating these words or answering affirmatively with, "I do," "Yes" or similar words. A nod or grunt is not a clear and sufficient response. If a person is mute and unable to speak, the Notary may rely on written notes to communicate.

Ceremony and Gestures. To impress upon the oath-taker or affirmant the importance of truthfulness, the Notary is encouraged to lend a sense of ceremony and formality to the oath or affirmation. During administration of the oath or affirmation, the Notary and the document signer traditionally raise their right hands, though this is not a legal requirement. Notaries generally have discretion to use words and gestures they feel will most compellingly appeal to the conscience of the oath-taker or affirmant.

'Artificial Persons' Not Sworn. Only an individual may take an oath (or affirmation). An "artificial person" such as a corporation or a partnership may not take an oath.

Personal Appearance Required. An oath (or affirmation) may not be given over the telephone. The oath-taker must physically appear in front of the Notary. In addition, a Notary may not administer an oath (or affirmation) to himself or herself.

Proof of Execution by Subscribing Witness

Purpose. In executing a proof of execution by subscribing witness, a Notary certifies that the signature of a person who does not appear before the Notary — the principal signer — is genuine and freely made based on the sworn testimony of another person who does appear, — the subscribing (signing) witness.

Proofs of execution are used when the principal signer is out of town or otherwise unavailable to appear before a Notary. Due to their high potential for fraudulent abuse, proofs of execution are not universally accepted.

Although literature issued by the Michigan Department of State suggests that a Notary should not accept a signature based on the word of a third party, Michigan law does state that proofs may be performed (MCL 565.262).

However, prudence dictates that proofs only be used as a last resort and never merely because the principal signer prefers not to take the time to personally appear before a Notary.

In Lieu of Acknowledgment. On recordable documents, a proof of execution by a subscribing witness is usually regarded as an acceptable substitute for an acknowledgment (MCL 565.262).

Subscribing Witness. A subscribing witness is a person who watches a principal sign a document (or who personally takes the principal's acknowledgment) and then subscribes (signs) his or her own name on the document at the principal's request. This witness brings that document to a Notary on the principal's behalf and takes an oath or affirmation from the Notary to the effect that the principal is known to him or her, and did indeed willingly sign (or acknowledge signing) the document and request the witness to also sign the document.

The ideal subscribing witness personally knows the principal signer and has no personal beneficial or financial interest in the document or transaction. It would be foolish of the Notary, for example, to rely on the word of a subscribing witness presenting for notarization a power of attorney that names this very witness as attorney in fact.

Identifying Subscribing Witness. Since the Notary is relying entirely upon the word of the subscribing witness to vouch for an absent signer's identity, willingness and general competency, it is best for subscribing witnesses to be personally known to the Notary.

Certificate for Proof of Execution. Michigan statute does not prescribe a notarial certificate for a proof of execution by a subscribing witness. When wording is not provided, the National Notary Association recommends the following format for a proof of execution by a subscribing witness:

State of Michigan)
) ss.
County of ________)

On ________ (date), before me, the undersigned, a Notary Public for the state, personally appeared ________ (subscribing witness's name), personally known to me to be the person whose name is subscribed to the within instrument, as a witness thereto, who, being by me duly sworn, deposes and says that he/she was present and saw ________ (name of principal), the same person described in and whose name is subscribed to the within and annexed instrument in his/her authorized capacity(ies) as a party thereto, execute the same, and that said affiant subscribed his/her name to the within instrument as a witness at the request of ________ (name of principal).

Notary's Stamp________ Notary's Signature________

(If not in stamp, print or type Notary's name; "Notary Public, State of Michigan, County of ________;" "My commission expires ________;" if acting in another county other than the county of commissioning, "Acting in the County of ________;" and the date the notarial act was performed.)

Witnessing or Attesting of Signatures

Purpose. The act of witnessing (or "attesting") a signature is similar to a jurat, except that it does not require the signer to take an oath or affirmation. It is used when establishing that the signing date is a major importance.

In witnessing or attesting a signature, the Notary certifies that (MCL 55.285[4]):

1) The signer personally appeared before the Notary on the date and in the county indicated on the notarial certificate.

2) The signer was positively identified by personally knowledge or satisfactory evidence.

3) The signer singed the document in the presence of the Notary.

Certificate. Michigan laws do no prescribe certificate wording, however the following wording is recommended:

State of Michigan)
County of ________)

Signed or attested before me on ______ (date) by ____ (name of person appearing).

___________ (Signature of Notary) (Seal of Notary)

___________ (Commission Number and Expiration Date)
___________ (Notary Printed Name)
___________ (County where Appointed)

Wills

May Only Notarize if Wording is Provided. Michigan law does not directly address notarization of wills, but state officials advise that a Notary should notarize a document described as a will only if a notarial certificate is provided or stipulated for each signer, and the signers are not asking questions about how to proceed. Any such questions should be answered by an attorney.

Foreign-Language Documents

Although Michigan law does not directly address the notarization of documents written in a language other than English, there are difficulties and dangers in notarizing a document that the Notary cannot understand.

The foremost danger is that the document may have been misrepresented to the Notary. Ideally, documents in foreign languages should be referred to Notaries who can read these languages; in large cities, such multilingual Notaries are often found in ethnic neighborhoods or in foreign consulates.

If a Notary chooses to notarize a document that he or she cannot read, at the very least the notarial certificate should be in English, or in a language the Notary can read. (See "Foreign Languages," page 57.)

PRACTICES AND PROCEDURES

Identifying Document Signers

Three Identification Methods. In notarizing a signature on any document, Michigan law requires the Notary to identify the acknowledger. The following three methods of identification are acceptable (MCL 55.285):

1) The Notary's *personal knowledge* of the signer's identity (see "Personal Knowledge of Identity," page 39);

2) The oath or affirmation of a personally known *credible identifying witness* (see "Credible Identifying Witnesses," pages 39–40); or

3) Reliable *identification documents* or ID cards (see "Identification Documents," pages 40–42).

The latter two methods of identification — credible witnesses and identification documents — are regarded as "satisfactory evidence" of identity.

Personal Knowledge of Identity

The safest and most reliable method of identifying a document signer is for the Notary to depend on his or her own personal knowledge of the signer's identity. Personal knowledge means familiarity with an individual resulting from interactions with that person over a period of time sufficient to eliminate every reasonable doubt that the person has the identity claimed. The familiarity should come from association with the individual in relation to other people and should be based upon a chain of circumstances surrounding the individual.

Michigan law does not specify how long a Notary must be acquainted with an individual before personal knowledge of identity may be claimed, so the Notary's common sense must prevail. In general, the longer the Notary is acquainted with a person, and the more random interactions the Notary has had with that person, the more likely the individual is indeed personally known.

For instance, the Notary might safely regard a friend since childhood as personally known, but would be foolish to consider a person met for the first time the previous day as such. Whenever the Notary has a reasonable doubt about a signer's identity, that individual should be considered not personally known, and the identification should be made through either a credible identifying witness or reliable identification documents.

Credible Identifying Witness

Purpose. When a document signer is not personally known to the Notary and is not able to present reliable ID cards, that signer may be identified on the oath (or affirmation) of a credible identifying witness (MCL 55.285[6][b]).

Qualifications. Every credible identifying witness should personally know the document signer. The credible identifying witness should also be personally known by the Notary. This establishes a "chain of personal knowledge" from the Notary to the credible identifying witness to the signer. In a sense, a credible identifying witness is a walking, talking ID card.

Credible identifying witnesses must never themselves be identified to the Notary through ID cards. Any credible identifying witness should have a reputation for honesty; the witness should be a competent, independent individual who won't be tricked, cajoled, bullied or otherwise influenced into identifying someone he or she does not really know. In addition, the witness should have no direct personal interest in the transaction requiring a notarial act.

Oath (or Affirmation) for Credible Identifying Witness. To ensure truthfulness, the Notary must administer an oath or affirmation to each credible identifying witness.

If not otherwise prescribed by Michigan law, an acceptable credible-witness oath or affirmation might be:

> Do you solemnly swear that you know that the signer is the person he/she claims to be, so help you God?
>
> (Do you solemnly affirm that you know that the signer is the person he/she claims to be?)

Signature in Notary's Journal. If the Notary maintains a journal — although a journal is not required by Michigan law — each credible identifying witness should sign the Notary's journal, along with the document signer. The Notary should also print each witness's name and address.

Not a Subscribing Witness. Do not confuse *credible identifying* witness with *subscribing* witness. A credible identifying witness vouches for the identity of a signer who appears before the Notary. A subscribing witness vouches for the genuineness of the signature of a person who does not appear before the Notary. (See "Proof of Execution by Subscribing Witness," pages 35–37.)

Identification Documents (ID Cards)

Acceptable Identification Documents. Michigan Notaries are allowed to use a current license, identification card or record issued by a federal or state government and containing the person's photograph and signature to identify document signers whom they do not personally know (MCL 55.285[6][b]).

The best ID cards have an additional component: a physical description (e.g., "brown hair, green eyes," etc.) of the bearer. Such ID cards are considered to be "satisfactory evidence" of identity in lieu of personal knowledge, just as is the sworn word of a personally known credible identifying witness (Public Act 238 of '03, Sect. 25[6]).

Acceptable forms of identification include:

- Michigan driver's license or official nondriver's ID.
- U.S. and foreign passports.
- U.S. military ID.
- Resident alien ID, or "green card," issued by the U.S. Citizenship and Immigration Services (USCIS).

Multiple Identification. While one good identification document or card may be sufficient to identify a signer, the Notary is encouraged to ask for more.

Unacceptable Identification Documents. Unacceptable ID cards for identifying signers include Social Security cards, credit cards and birth certificates. Acceptable IDs must be current, government-issued and bear both a photograph and signature.

Fraudulent Identification. Identification documents are the least secure of the three methods of identifying a document signer, because phony ID cards are common. The Notary should scrutinize each card for evidence of tampering or counterfeiting, or for evidence that it is a genuine card that has been issued to an impostor.

Some clues that an ID card may have been fraudulently tampered with include: mismatched type styles, a photograph with a raised surface, a signature that does not match the signature on the document and unauthorized lamination of the card. Smudges, erasures, smears and discolorations may also be clues.

Possible tip-offs to a counterfeit ID card include: misspelled words, a brand new-looking card with an old date of issuance, two cards with exactly the same photograph showing the bearer in identical clothing or with an identical background and inappropriate patterns and features.

Some possible indications that a card may have been issued to an impostor include: the birth date or address on the card is unfamiliar to the bearer, all the ID cards seem brand new and the bearer is unwilling to leave a thumbprint in the journal. (Such a print is not required by law but is requested by some Notaries as protection against forgers and lawsuits. Refusal to leave a thumbprint is not in itself grounds to deny a notarization.)

Journal of Notarial Acts

Recommended. Michigan law does not directly address the requirement of maintaining a journal. However, state officials strongly recommend that each time a Notary performs a notarial act, he or she should record the signer's name, identification, date of notarization and any additional pertinent information in a recordbook.

Of course, the National Notary Association and many Notary-regulating officials across the nation strongly endorse the policy of keeping a journal of all notarial acts as both protection for the public and the Notary.

Prudent Notaries keep detailed and accurate journals of their notarial acts for many reasons:

- Keeping records is a *businesslike practice* that every conscientious businessperson and public official should engage in. Not keeping records of important transactions, whether private or public, is risky.

- A Notary's recordbook *protects the public's rights* to valuable property and to due process by providing documentary evidence in the event a document is lost or altered, or if a transaction is later challenged.

- In the event of a civil lawsuit alleging that the Notary's negligence or misconduct caused the plaintiff serious financial harm, a detailed journal of notarial acts can *protect the Notary* by showing that reasonable care was used to identify a signer. It would be difficult to contend that the Notary did not bother to identify a signer if the Notary's journal contains a detailed description of the ID cards that the signer presented.

- Since civil lawsuits arising from a contested notarial act typically take place three to six years after the act occurs, the Notary normally cannot accurately testify in court about the particulars of a notarization without a journal to *aid the Notary's memory.*

- Journals of notarial acts *prevent or abort baseless lawsuits* by showing that a Notary did use reasonable care, or that a transaction did occur as recorded. Journal fingerprints and signatures are especially effective in defeating such groundless suits.

- Requiring each document signer to leave a signature, or even a fingerprint, in the Notary's journal both *deters attempted forgeries* and provides strong evidence for a conviction should a forgery occur.

Journal Entries. The Notary's recordbook should contain the following information for each notarial act performed:

1) The date, time of day and type of notarization (e.g., jurat, acknowledgment, etc.).

2) The type (or title) of document notarized (e.g., deed of trust, affidavit of support, etc.), including the number of pages and the date of the document.

3) The signature, address and printed name of each document signer and witness.

4) A statement as to how the signer's identity was confirmed. (If by personal knowledge, the journal entry should read "Personal Knowledge." If by other satisfactory evidence, the journal entry should contain either: a description of the ID card accepted, including the type of ID, the government agency issuing the ID, the serial or identifying number and the date of issuance or expiration; the signature and address of any credible identifying witness — see "Credible Identifying Witness," pages 39–40.)

5) Any other pertinent information, including the fee charged for the notarial service, the capacity of the signer (e.g., president of XYZ Company) or any other significant peculiarities relating to the signer or the document.

Journal Thumbprint. Increasingly, Notaries are asking document signers to leave a thumbprint in the journal. The journal thumbprint is a strong deterrent to forgery, because it represents absolute proof of the forger's identity and appearance before the Notary. Nothing prevents a Notary from asking for a thumbprint for every notarial act, if the signer is willing. However, the Notary may not make leaving a thumbprint a precondition for notarizing.

Completing the Entry. The prudent Notary completes the journal or recordbook entry before filling out the notarial certificate on a document. This prevents the signer from suddenly leaving with the notarized document before vital information can be entered in the journal or recordbook.

Never Surrender Journal. Notaries should never surrender control of their journals to anyone, unless expressly subpoenaed by a court order. Even when an employer has paid for the Notary's official journal and seal, they go with the Notary upon termination of employment. No person but the Notary may properly possess and use these records.

Responding to Secretary's Request to Inspect. Within 15 days after receiving a written or electronic request from the Michigan Secretary of State, the Notary must allow inspection or provide pertinent copies of his or her journal — and keep this information accessible for at least five years after the date of the last notarial act (MCL 55.295).

For failure to respond to such a request, the Secretary may indefinitely suspend the Notary's commission (MCL 55.295[2]).

Notarial Certificate

Requirement. In notarizing any document, a Notary must complete a notarial certificate. The certificate is wording that indicates exactly what the Notary has certified or attested to. The notarial certificate may be either preprinted or typed on the document itself or added as an attachment to it. The certificate should contain (MCL 55.289[3-10]):

1) A *venue* indicating where the notarization is being performed. "State of Michigan, County of __________," is the typical venue wording, with the county name inserted in the blank. The letters "SS." or "SCT." sometimes appear after the venue; they abbreviate the traditional Latin word scilicet, meaning "in particular" or "namely."

2) A *statement of particulars* which indicates what the notarization has attested. An acknowledgment certificate

might include such wording as: "On __________ (date) before me, __________ (name of Notary), personally appeared, __________ (name of signer), personally known to me (or proved to me on the basis of satisfactory evidence) to be the person(s) ..." A jurat certificate would include such wording as: "Subscribed and sworn to (or affirmed) before me this _______ (date) by __________ (name of signer)."

3) A *testimonium clause*, which may be optional if the date is included in the statement of particulars: "Witness my hand and official seal, this the ____ day of __________ (month), ____ (year)." In this short sentence, the Notary formally attests to the truthfulness of the preceding facts in the certificate. "Hand" means signature.

4) The *official signature of the Notary*, exactly as the name appears on the Notary's commission application.

5) The *seal of the Notary*, although not required by Michigan law. On many certificates the letters "L.S." appear, indicating where the seal is to be located. These letters abbreviate the Latin term *locus sigilli*, meaning "place of the seal." An inking seal should be placed near but not over the letters, so that wording imprinted by the seal will not be obscured. An embossing seal, used in conjunction with an inking seal, may be placed directly over the letters — slightly displacing portions of the characters and leaving a clue that document examiners can use to distinguish an original from a forged photocopy.

6) Additional information may be required if it is not included in the Notary seal. Michigan requires the Notary to type, print or stamp the Notary's name, title ("Notary Public") and commission expiration date, the name of the state and county in which the Notary is commissioned, the date the notarial act was performed and, if notarizing in a county other than the county of commissioning, the name of the county in which the notarial act was performed (MCL 55.287).

Loose Certificates. When certificate wording is not preprinted on the document for the Notary to fill out, a "loose" certificate may be attached. Normally, this form is stapled to the document's left margin preceding or following the signature page. Only one side of the certificate should be stapled, so it can be lifted to show the document underneath.

To prevent a loose certificate from being removed and fraudulently placed on another document, there are precautions a Notary can take. The Notary can emboss the certificate and document together, writing, "Attached document bears embossment," on the certificate. Or the Notary can write a brief description of the document on the certificate: e.g., "This certificate is attached to a __________ (title or type of document), dated __________, of __________ (number) pages, also signed by __________ (name[s] of other signer[s])."

While fraud-deterrent steps such as these can make it much more difficult for a loose certificate to be removed and misused, there is no absolute protection against its removal and misuse. Notaries must absolutely ensure that while a certificate remains in their control, it is attached only to its intended document.

<u>Do Not Pre-Sign/Seal Certificates</u>. A Notary should never sign and/or seal certificates ahead of time or permit other persons to attach loose notarial certificates to documents. Nor should the Notary send an unattached, signed and sealed, loose certificate through the mail, even if requested to do so by a signer who previously appeared before the Notary. These actions may facilitate fraud or forgery, and they could subject the Notary to lawsuits to recover damages resulting from the Notary's neglect or misconduct.

<u>Selecting Certificates</u>. It is not the role of the Notary to decide what type of certificate — thus, what type of notarization — a document needs. As ministerial officials, Notaries generally follow instructions and fill out forms that have been provided for them; they do not issue instructions and decide which forms are appropriate in a given case.

If a document is presented to a Notary without certificate wording and if the signer doesn't know what type of notarization is appropriate, the signer should be asked to find out what kind of notarization and certificate are needed. Usually, the agency that issued the document, or that will be accepting the document, can provide this information. Selecting certificates may be regarded as the unauthorized practice of law.

False Certificates. A Notary who knowingly completes a false notarial certificate may be subject to civil and criminal penalties. A Notary would be completing a false certificate, for example, if he or she signed and sealed an acknowledgment certificate indicating a signer personally appeared when the signer actually did not.

Notary Seal

Optional. Michigan law does not require Notaries to use seals of office, but statutes do stipulate that a Notary must type, print or stamp, in addition to his or her official signature, the Notary's name, title ("Notary Public") and commission expiration date, the name of the state and county in which the Notary is commissioned, the date the notarial act was performed and, if notarizing in a county other than the county of commissioning, the name of the county in which the notarial act was performed (MCL 55.287).

Many Notaries elect to use seals to impart an appropriate sense of ceremony to their official acts. Another very practical reason for using a Notary seal on notarized documents sent to other states and nations: the absence of a seal may delay or, on occasion in foreign nations, prevent the document's acceptance.

Embossing and Inking Seals. There are two types of Notary seal: the traditional metal embosser, which crimps its impression onto a paper surface; and the more modern inking stamp, usually with a rubber face, which imprints a photocopiable impression on the paper.

County recording officials prefer inking seals because they considerably simplify the process of microfilming property deeds and other recordable documents. Recorders have to smudge seal embossments with carbon or other photocopiable substances before they can be microfilmed. Michigan law prohibits use of an embosser Notary seal by itself because it is not photocopiable (MCL 55.287[3]).

Required Information. On every notarial certificate, a Notary must type, print or stamp the Notary's name, title ("Notary Public") and commission expiration date, the name of the state and county in which the Notary is commissioned, the date the notarial act was performed and, if notarizing in a county other than the county of commissioning, the name of the county in which the notarial act was performed (MCL 55.287).

Placement of Seal Impression. The Notary's seal impression should be placed near the Notary's signature on the notarial certificate. Whenever possible — and especially with documents that will be submitted to a public recorder — the Notary should not affix the seal over any text on the document or certificate.

Some recorders will reject documents if writing or document text intrudes within the borders of the Notary's seal. If there is no room for a seal, the Notary may have no choice but to complete and attach a loose certificate that duplicates the notarial wording on the document.

With documents that will not be publicly recorded, however, the recipient may allow the Notary to affix the seal over boilerplate text — the standard preprinted clauses or sections — as long as the wording within the seal is not obscured.

L.S. The letters "L.S." — from the Latin *locus sigilli*, meaning "location of the seal" — appear on many notarial certificates to indicate where the Notary seal should be placed. Only an embosser seal, used in addition to an inking seal, should be placed over these letters. The inking seal should be placed near, but not over, the letters.

Fees for Notarial Services

Maximum Fees. For any notarial act — acknowledgment, jurat, administering an oath or affirmation or witnessing or attesting a signature — a maximum fee of $10 is allowed by Michigan law (MCL 55.285[7]).

Inform Before Notarization. Before performing any notarial act, the Notary must inform the signer of the fees, either through a "conspicuous" sign or through expressly advising the person (MCL 55.285[7]).

Travel Fees. Michigan law does not set maximum travel fees for Notaries, but it does indicate that the Notary should inform the constituent in advance if a travel fee is going to be charged and the signer should agree to the amount. The Notary should take care to clarify that such travel fee is separate from the actual notarization fee (MCL 55.285[7]).

Overcharging. Charging more than the legally prescribed fees may subject the Notary to:

- Denial, suspension or revocation of the Notary commission.

- A fine of not more than $1,000.

- A letter of censure.

- A requirement to pay restitution to an injured person or to take other affirmative action.

- A requirement to reimburse the Secretary of State for the costs of the investigation (MCL 55.300a[1][f]).

Blank or Incomplete Documents

Do Not Notarize. While Michigan no longer prohibits notarizing blank or incomplete documents, this is a dangerous, unbusinesslike practice and a breach of common sense, similar to signing a blank check.

A fraudulent document could readily be created above a Notary's signed and sealed certificate on an otherwise blank paper. And, with documents containing blanks to be filled in after the notarization by a person other than the signer, there is a danger that the information inserted will be contrary to the wishes of the signer.

Any blanks in a document should be filled in by the signer. If the blanks are inapplicable and intended to be left unfilled, the signer should be asked to line through each space (using ink) or write "not applicable" or "N/A."

False Documents

Notary Not Responsible. It is not the duty of the Notary to verify the truthfulness or accuracy of the facts in the text of a document. In fact, Notaries are not even required to read the documents they notarize. The Notary is entitled, though, to quickly scan the instrument to extract important particulars (its title, date and number of pages, for example) to record in an official recordbook.

However, if a Notary happens to discover that a document is false or fraudulent, the Notary, as a responsible public official, has a duty to refuse the notarization and to report the attempted fraud to appropriate authorities.

Disqualifying Interest

Impartiality. Notaries are appointed by the state to be impartial, disinterested witnesses whose screening duties help ensure the integrity of important legal and commercial transactions. Lack of impartiality by a Notary throws doubt on the integrity and lawfulness of any transaction. A Notary must never notarize his or her own signature or notarize a transaction to which the Notary is a party or in which the Notary has a financial or beneficial interest (MCL 55.291[7-8]).

Financial or Beneficial Interest. A financial or beneficial interest exists when the Notary is individually named as a principal in a financial transaction or when the Notary receives an advantage, right, privilege, property or fee valued in excess of the lawfully prescribed notarial fee.

According to Michigan law, a Notary must not notarize if the Notary is named individually in a transaction as a grantor, grantee, mortgagor, mortgagee, trustor, trustee, beneficiary, vendor, vendee, lessor, lessee or as a party to the transaction in some other capacity. These are also regarded as disqualifying conflicts of interest (MCL 55.291[7]).

Exemptions. Certain persons are exempt from this beneficial and financial interest provision. A Notary who is an agent, employee, insurer, attorney, escrow or lender for a person signing a document may notarize the document without being considered to have a disqualifying financial or beneficial interest. For example, a real estate agent can notarize a document relating to a property transfer even if the agent derives a commission from that transaction (MCL 55.291[11]).

Corporations. A Michigan Notary who is a stockholder, director, officer, employee or agent of a bank or corporation may administer an oath to any other stockholder, director, officer, employee or agent of the bank or corporation. However, a Notary who is a stockholder, director, officer or employee of a bank or corporation may not notarize a document if he or she is named as a party to that document (MCL 55.291[10]).

Relatives. State laws prohibit a Notary from notarizing for a lineal ancestor. "Lineal ancestor" is defined as an individual in the direct line of ascent including, but not limited to, a parent or grandparent because of the likelihood of a financial or beneficial interest (MCL 55.291[8]).

It is often difficult for a Notary to retain impartiality with a close friend or relative. Anyone, for example, is entitled to counsel a parent to sign or not to sign an important document, but such counseling is entirely inappropriate for the impartial Notary.

Family members, even those not specifically prohibited by law, should seek a third party Notary to avoid any question of a disqualifying interest.

Refusal of Services

Legal Requests for Services. Notaries should honor all lawful and reasonable requests to notarize. In addition, a person's race, advanced age, gender, religion, nationality, ethnicity, lifestyle, politics or the Notary's personal bias are not due cause for refusing to perform a notarial act.

Noncustomer Discrimination Prohibited. As a public official, a Notary employed by a private employer should not discriminate between customers and noncustomers. Fees and services provided should be the same for all customers, whether or not the customer is a client of the employer.

Penalty. Should a Notary refuse to perform a notarial act when lawfully requested, the Notary may be subject to charges of official misconduct. Such misconduct may subject the Notary to removal from office (MCL 55.297).

Exception. A Notary may refuse to notarize a document if he or she knows that the document is blatantly fraudulent.

Reasonable Care

Responsibility. As public servants, Notaries must act responsibly and exercise reasonable care in the performance of their official duties. If a Notary fails to do so, he or she may be subject to a civil suit to recover financial damages caused by the Notary's error or omission.

In general, reasonable care is that degree of concern and attentiveness that a person of normal intelligence and responsibility would exhibit. If a Notary can demonstrate to a judge or jury that he or she did everything expected of a reasonable person, the judge or jury is obligated by law to find the Notary blameless and not liable for damages.

Complying with all pertinent laws is the first rule of reasonable care for a Notary. And, if there are no statutory guidelines in a given instance, the Notary should go to extremes to use common sense and prudence. (See "Steps to Proper Notarization," pages 14–18.)

Records. Although not required by law, a Notary's best proof of having exercised reasonable care is a detailed, accurate journal of notarial acts. Such entries as the serial numbers of ID cards and the signatures of credible identifying witnesses can show that the Notary took steps to positively identify every signer. Possession by the Notary of a well-maintained recordbook can prevent lawsuits that falsely claim the Notary was negligent.

Unauthorized Practice of Law

Do Not Assist in Legal Matters. A Notary may not give legal advice or accept fees for legal advice. As a ministerial official, the nonattorney Notary is generally not permitted to assist other persons in drafting, preparing, selecting, completing or understanding a document or transaction.

The Notary should not fill in the blank spaces in the text of a document for other persons, tell others what documents they need or how to draft them, nor advise others about the legal sufficiency of a document — and especially not for a fee.

A Notary, of course, may fill in the blanks on the portion of any document containing the notarial certificate. As a private individual, a Notary may prepare legal documents that he or she is personally a party to; but the Notary may not then notarize his or her own signature on these same documents.

Do Not Determine Notarial Act. A Notary who is not an attorney may not determine the type of notarial act to perform or decide which certificate to attach. This is beyond the scope of the Notary's expertise and might be considered the unauthorized practice of law. The Notary should only follow instructions provided by the document, its signer, its issuing or receiving agency or an attorney.

If a document lacks notarial certificate wording, the Notary must ask the document signer what type of notarization — acknowledgment, jurat or signature witnessing — is required. The Notary may then type the appropriate notarial wording on the document or attach a preprinted, loose certificate. If the signer does not know what type of notarization is required, the issuing or receiving agency should be contacted. This decision is never to be made by the Notary, unless the Notary is also an attorney.

Exceptions. Specially trained, nonattorney Notaries certified or licensed in a particular field (e.g., real estate, insurance, escrow, etc.) may offer advice or prepare documents related to that field only. Paralegals under the supervision of an attorney may give advice about documents in routine legal matters.

Signature by Mark

Mark Serves as Signature. A person who cannot sign his or her name because of illiteracy or a physical disability may instead use a mark — an "X," for example — as a signature, as long as there are two witnesses to the making of the mark.

Witnesses. For a signature by mark to be notarized, there must be two witnesses to the making of the mark. Although a Michigan Notary is permitted to witness and notarize the same document, it is recommended that the two witnesses be in addition to the Notary.

Both witnesses should sign the document and the Notary's journal. As shown below, one witness should print legibly the marker's name beside the mark on the document. It is recommended that a mark also be affixed in the Notary's journal.

In the presence of: ________________
Jane Doe

his
JOHN X JONES
mark

Notarization Procedures. Because a properly witnessed mark is considered a signature under custom and law, no special notarial certificate is required. As required of any other signer, the marker must be positively identified.

Disabled Signers

Notary as Proxy Signer. A Notary may sign any document on behalf of a signer who, due to physical disability, cannot execute a document without assistance (MCL 55.293).

Direction by Signer. The Notary must be directed to sign by the person by oral, written, electronic or mechanical means — such as an electronic communication device for persons unable to speak (MCL 55.293).

Personal Appearance Required. As with other types of notarization, an individual seeking assistance with signing a document must be in the physical presence of the Notary when the Notary signs on his or her behalf (MCL 55.293).

Required Information. In addition to the usual required notarial certificate information, the Notary must inscribe beneath the signature he or she made on behalf of the signer, "Signature affixed pursuant to section 33 of the Michigan Notary Public Act," (MCL 55.293).

Notarizing for Minors

Under Age 18. Generally, persons must reach the age of majority before they can handle their own legal affairs and sign documents for themselves. In Michigan, the age of majority is 18. Normally, natural guardians (parents) or court-appointed guardians will sign on a minor's behalf. In certain cases, where minors are engaged in business transactions or serving as court witnesses, they may lawfully sign documents on their own behalves and have their signatures notarized.

Include Age Next to Signature. When notarizing for a minor, the Notary should ask the young signer to write his or her age next to the signature to alert any person relying on the document that the signer is a minor. The Notary is not required to verify the minor signer's age.

Identification. The method for identifying a minor is the same as that for an adult. However, determining the identity of a minor can be a problem, because minors often do not possess acceptable identification documents such as driver's licenses or passports. If the minor does not have acceptable ID, then the other methods of identifying acknowledgers must be used, either the Notary's personal knowledge of the minor or the oath of a credible identifying witness who can identify the minor. (See "Credible Identifying Witness," pages 39–40.)

Authentication

Documents Sent Out of State. Documents notarized in Michigan and sent to other states or nations may be required to bear proof that the Notary's signature and seal are genuine and that the Notary had authority to act at the time of notarization. This process of proving the genuineness of an official signature and seal is called *authentication* or *legalization*.

In Michigan, the proof is in the form of an authenticating certificate attached to the notarized document by either the county clerk's office where the Notary has been appointed or the Department of State (MCL 565.263).

Certificate. These authenticating certificates are known by different names: certificates of authority, certificates of capacity, certificates of authenticity, certificates of prothonotary and "flags."

In sending a notarized document from Michigan to another nation, attachment of an authenticating certificate from the Department of State may be necessary in addition to or in lieu of the county clerk's certificate (MCL 565.263).

Procedure. An individual seeking to obtain an authentication certificate through the mail should include a cover letter with the name, address and telephone number of the person making the request.

Contact either the specific clerk of the county in which the Notary has filed an oath and bond or one of the Department of State offices at:

Regular Mail ($1):
Office of the Great Seal
7064 Crowner Blvd.
Lansing, MI 48918

Walk-in or Courier Service ($1 plus
courier fee and prepaid postage):
Office of the Great Seal
Richard H. Austin Building 1st Floor
430 W. Allegan Street
Lansing, MI 48915
Telephone: (888) 767-6424

Depending on the type of mail service requested, issuance of the authentication certificates takes approximately three days to three weeks. Same-day service is available by personally appearing at the second office listed above. No appointment is necessary, but prearrangement is required when requesting certificates for five or more documents. Contact the Department at (517) 373-2531 to prearrange service. If requesting authentication from a county, the individual should visit the office of the county clerk in the particular county. (See the list of county clerks, pages 94–97.)

Documents Sent Out of Country. If the notarized document is going out of the United States, a "chain" authentication process may be necessary. Additional certificates of authority may have to be obtained from the U.S. Department of State in Washington, D.C., a foreign consulate in Washington, D.C. and a ministry of foreign affairs in the particular foreign nation.

Apostilles and the Hague Convention. Fortunately, over 90 nations, including the United States, subscribe to a treaty under the auspices of the Hague Conference. This treaty simplifies authentication of notarized documents exchanged between any of the participating nations. The official name of this treaty, adopted by the Conference on October 5, 1961, is the *Hague Convention Abolishing the Requirement of Legalization for Foreign Public Documents*. For a list of the subscribing countries, see "Hague Convention Nations," pages 102–104.

Under the Hague Convention, only one authenticating certificate, called an *apostille*, is necessary to ensure acceptance in these subscribing countries. (*Apostille* is French for "notation".) It is not necessary to obtain an authentication certificate from the county prior to requesting an *apostille*.

In Michigan, *apostilles* are issued by the Department of State's office (listed on page 55) for a $1 fee per authenticating certificate. *Apostilles* are not obtainable from the county clerk.

An *apostille* may be requested in writing by a letter including the name, address and telephone number of the person making the request. The letter must also identify the nation to which the document will be sent. A person requesting the *apostille* should send the letter, the notarized document and the appropriate fee to the Department of State office listed above.

Same-day service is available by personally appearing at the office listed above. No appointment is necessary, but prearrangement is required when requesting *apostilles* for five or more documents. Contact the Department at (517) 335-8656 to prearrange service.

It is *not* the Notary's responsibility to obtain an *apostille* but, rather, it is the responsibility of the party sending the document.

Documents From Other States and Nations. Michigan recognizes the validity of properly authenticated acknowledgments and proofs taken in other U.S. states, territories and districts by Notaries and other authorized officials, including (MCL 565.262):

- A judge, clerk or deputy clerk of a court in the place where the notarization is being performed.

- An officer of the foreign service of the United States or a consular agent.

- A commissioned officer in active service with the armed forces of the United States. (See "Military Officer Notarizations," pages 58–59.)

Foreign Languages

Foreign-Language Documents. Michigan Notaries are not prohibited from notarizing non-English documents. As long as the notarial certificate and document signature are in English or in a language the Notary can read and understand, Michigan Notaries may notarize foreign-language documents.

Although it is not expressly illegal to notarize a document written in a language the Notary cannot understand, there are difficulties and dangers in doing so. A blatant fraud might be undetectable; the U.S. Notary seal might be misinterpreted in another country; and making a journal entry might be difficult.

Ideally, documents in foreign languages should be referred to Notaries who read these languages; in large cities, such multilingual Notaries are often found in foreign consulates.

Foreign-Speaking Signers. There always should be direct communication between the Notary and document signer — whether in English or any other language. The Notary should never rely on an intermediary or interpreter to determine a signer's willingness or competence. A third party may have a motive for misrepresenting the circumstances to the Notary and/or signer.

Advertising Practices

False or Misleading Advertising. The use of false or misleading advertising by a Notary to represent that he or she has duties, rights and privileges not given by law may subject the Notary to charges of official misconduct and removal from office (MCL 55.291[3]).

Translation of "Notary Public". The nonattorney Notary is prohibited from using the literal translation from English into another language of such terms as Notary Public, Notary, licensed, attorney, lawyer or any other term that implies the person is an attorney. This applies to any document, advertisement, stationery, letterhead, business card or any other material describing the role of the Notary Public (MCL 55.291[4]).

Foreign-language Advertising. If a nonattorney Notary advertises notarial services in a language other than English, the Notary must also display the following prominently in the same language as the advertisement the statement: "I am not an attorney and have no authority to give advice on immigration or other legal matters." The Notary fees as specified by statute must also be included (MCL 55.291[5]).

"Notario Publico". Notaries are prohibited from using the term *"Notario Publico"* or any equivalent non-English term in any business card, advertisement, notice or sign (MCL 55. 291[6]).

Immigration

Do Not Give Advice. Nonattorney Notaries may never advise others on the subject of immigration, nor help others prepare immigration documents — especially not for a fee. Notaries who offer immigration advice to others may be subject to penalties for the unauthorized practice of law.

Documents. Certain immigration documents may be notarized. Affidavits issued or accepted by the U.S. Citizenship and Immigration Services (USCIS) are most often notarized, with the "Affidavit of Support" (Form I-134) being the most common.

Non-USCIS-issued documents are often notarized and submitted in support of an immigration petition. These may include translator's declarations, statements from employers and banks and affidavits of relationship.

If there appears to be no room for the Notary seal, if used, on an USCIS-issued document, federal officials advise that the stamp may be affixed over boilerplate text (standard clauses or sections).

Naturalization Certificates. A Notary may only photocopy a certificate of naturalization for lawful purposes. The NNA recommends a Notary only certify a copy of the certificate if written directions are provided by a U.S. immigration authority.

Military Officer Notarizations

May Notarize Worldwide. Certain U.S. military personnel may notarize anywhere in the world for other military personnel and certain associated groups, as stipulated by the U.S. Code, Title 10, Subtitle A, Part II, Chapter 53, Section 1044a(b). Based on that code, the following persons are authorized to act as Notaries:

- Judge advocates, including reserve judge advocates when not in a duty status
- Civilian attorneys serving as legal assistance attorneys
- Adjutants, assistant adjutants and personnel adjutants, including reserve members when not in a duty status
- Other members of the armed forces, including reserve members when not in a duty status, so authorized by armed-forces regulations or by statute

Validity of Notarial Acts. The signature of any of the above when acting as a Notary, together with the title of that individual's office, is considered proof that the signature is genuine, that the individual holds the designated title and that he or she is authorized to perform notarial acts (USC Title 10, Section 1044a[d]).

Fees. Military-officer Notaries may not charge or receive a fee for performing a notarial act (USC Title 10, Section 1044a[c]).

Wills

Do Not Offer Advice. A Notary risks prosecution for the unauthorized practice of law in advising a signer how to proceed with a will. Ill-informed advice may adversely affect the affairs of the signer. The format of a will is dictated by strict laws, and any deviation may result in nullification. In some cases, holographic (handwritten) wills have actually been voided by notarization.

Living Wills. Documents popularly called "living wills" may be notarized. These are not actual wills but written statements of a signer's wishes concerning medical treatment in the event he or she is unable to issue instructions on his or her own behalf.

Special Circumstances. In some states, self-proving wills may require the signatures of the witnesses to be notarized. A Notary should notarize a document described as a will *only* if a notarial certificate is provided or stipulated for each signer, and the signers are not asking questions about how to proceed. Any such questions should be answered by an attorney.

Uniform Real Property Electronic Recording Act (URPERA)

Effective July 19, 2010, Michigan signed into law Senate Bill 791, enacting the URPERA, which authorizes county registers of deeds to electronically record electronic real property deeds, mortgages, releases and other documents affecting title to real property. The URPERA also permits a Notary to use an electronic signature in notarizing an electronic real property document without affixing an image of the Notary's official physical seal. In addition, the URPERA creates an Electronic Recording Commission comprised of eight members as specified by the statute to create technical standards for electronic recording in Michigan.

Weddings

Cannot Perform Ceremony. Michigan Notaries have no authority to "solemnize nuptials," unless they are also ministers. Only Notaries in Maine, South Carolina and Florida are empowered to perform marriages strictly by virtue of holding a notarial commission.

MISCONDUCT, FINES AND PENALTIES

Prohibited Acts

Misconduct Defined. "Official misconduct" means either exercising power or performing a duty in a way that is unauthorized, unlawful, abusive, negligent, reckless or injurious, or charging more than the maximum authorized by law or both (MCL 55.265[d]).

Liable for Fraud. A Notary found liable for damages resulting from fraud, misrepresentation or other violation is guilty of misconduct (MCL 55.300a[2][e]).

False or Misleading Advertising. The use of false or misleading advertising by a Notary to represent that he or she has duties, rights and privileges not given by law may subject the Notary to charges of official misconduct and removal from office (MCL 55.291[3] and 55.300a[2][f]).

Not Completing Acknowledgment. A Notary who fails to complete an acknowledgment at the time the Notary's seal and signature are affixed may be guilty of misconduct (MCL 55.300a[2][h]).

Not Administering Oath. Failure to administer a required oath or affirmation may be considered misconduct (MCL 55.300a[2][i]).

Unauthorized Practice of Law. A Notary who advises or assists in drafting, preparing or completing legal documents or who offers advice to a signer about how to proceed may be guilty of misconduct (MCL 55.300a[2][j]).

Refuse Request for Records. Hindering or refusing a request by the Secretary of State for notarial records or papers is punishable as misconduct (MCL 55.300a[2][m]).

Unfair or Deceptive Practice. A Notary who engages in any practice that is unfair or deceptive, including misrepresenting the duties or responsibilities of a Notary, may be found guilty of misconduct (MCL 55.300a[2][n]).

Permitting Unlawful Use of Seal. A Notary who fails to safeguard the official seal and permits another to use it may be guilty of misconduct (MCL 55.300a[2][p]).

Failure of Duty. Failure to fully and faithfully discharge the duties or responsibilities of a Notary may subject the Notary to charges of official misconduct and removal from office (MCL 55.300a[2][d]).

Certify Copies and Originals. Michigan Notaries are specifically prohibited from certifying that a document is either an original or a copy of another record (MCL 55.291[1]).

Notarize Own Signature. Notaries are not permitted to notarize their own signatures or documents in which they are named. Likewise, Notaries may not take their own depositions or affidavits (MCL 55.291[2]).

Conflict of Interest. A Notary may not perform a notarial act in connection with a transaction if the Notary has a conflict of interest. This prohibits a Notary from notarizing if he or she is named as a grantor, grantee, mortgagor, mortgagee, trustor, trustee, beneficiary, vendor, vendee, lessor, lessee or as a party in any capacity to the transaction. A Notary with a direct beneficial or financial interest in a transaction, other than the Notary fee, is also prohibited from notarizing (MCL 55.291[7]).

A Notary is not considered to have a beneficial or financial interest in a transaction where the Notary acts as an agent, employee, insurer, attorney, escrow or lender for a document signer (MCL 55.291[11]).

Relatives. Michigan Notaries may not notarize for a lineal ancestor. "Lineal ancestor" is defined as an individual in the direct line of ascent including, but not limited to, a parent or grandparent (MCL 55.291[8]).

Overcharging. A Notary who charges more than the legally prescribed fees is guilty of misconduct (MCL55.265[d]).

False Acknowledgments. A Notary should ensure that a certificate for an acknowledgment reflects the date the signer actually appeared before the Notary. A certificate that indicates a different date than when the signer actually appeared is considered to be fraudulent.

False Certificate. A Notary who knowingly completes a false certificate may be subject to criminal penalties.

Telephone Acknowledgments. Michigan law does not directly address taking acknowledgments over the telephone, but it does expressly require document signers to personally appear before the Notary (MCL 565.266).

Undue Influence. Since Notaries are appointed to serve as impartial witnesses, a Notary never attempts to influence a person to execute or not to execute a document or transaction requiring a notarial act by that Notary.

Administrative Penalties

Misconduct. For any act of official misconduct by a Notary, the Department of State may impose any of the following penalties: suspension or revocation of the Notary's commission; denial of an application for appointment; a fine of not more than $1,000; mandatory affirmative action determined by the Secretary, including payment of restitution to an injured person; a letter of censure; and requirement to reimburse the Secretary's office for the cost of the investigation (MCL 55.300a[1]).

Application Misstatement. Substantial and material misstatement or omission of information in the application for a Notary commission may be reason for the Department of State to return the application to the would-be Notary until correction is made.

Falsely Acting as a Notary. Any person who is not a Notary and who represents himself or herself as a Notary Public and causes harm or damages to a private party may be subject to civil action by the injured party.

Unauthorized Practice of Law

Never Give Advice. Giving advice about a legal document when one is not a lawyer may be construed as the unauthorized practice of law and may be reason for the Department of State to suspend, revoke or refuse to grant a Notary's commission.

In addition to penalties imposed by the Department of State, the Supreme Court has the power to prosecute for criminal contempt any person who unlawfully practices or assumes to practice law.

A Notary cannot counsel or advise the drawing of agreements, the organization of corporations or the preparation of such papers. Notaries cannot draft legal documents of any kind, including wills.

In the rare case of drawing an affidavit at the direction of the signer, the Notary must take steps to avoid advising the signer.

Complaint and Investigation

Secretary May Investigate. The Secretary of State may investigate a Notary who has allegedly violated or is about to violate a statute or rule. Any individual may file a complaint against the Notary with the Secretary of State in a format containing: the complainant's name, address, telephone number and the complainant's signature; the date the complaint was signed; and a complete statement describing the basis for the complaint and the actual document or a copy of the document involved in the complaint (MCL 55.300).

Notary Must Respond to Request. If a Notary receives a written or electronic request from the Secretary of State requesting information, including a copy of the Notary's records or access to inspect the Notary's records, that Notary must comply within 15 days of receiving the request. Failure to respond may result in suspension of the Notary's commission until he or she does comply (MCL 55.295).

Right to a Hearing. Before the Secretary applies an administrative penalty, the Notary affected will be given notice and an opportunity for a hearing (MCL 55.300a[3]).

Civil Lawsuit

Liability for Damages. A Notary may be subject to civil actions for willful violations, including fraud and dishonesty.

Found Liable for Fraud or Misrepresentation. Being found liable for damages in a suit accusing fraud, misrepresentation or violation of state laws may be reason for the Department of State to charge the Notary with official misconduct and removal from office (MCL 55.300a[2][e]).

A Notary found guilty of such misconduct or negligence may also be subject to a civil lawsuit to recover damages.

Protection for Public. Michigan Notaries are required to hold a surety bond in the amount of $10,000. The bond is intended to protect the public against a Notary's negligence and misconduct (MCL 55.273[2]).

Protection for Notary. In some instances, a civil lawsuit against the Notary may seek financial recovery against any and all of the Notary's personal assets.

Errors and omissions insurance may provide limited protection to the accused Notary, but only for unintentional mistakes made while performing a notarial act. Errors and omissions insurance does not protect the Notary for negligence or intentional misconduct.

Felony

Performing Notarization After Commission Revoked. Effective January 1, 2012, House Bill 4492 sets a maximum sentence of five years for violation of Michigan Notary Public Act section 55.301, performing a notarial act while commission is revoked and a fine of $3,000 (MCL 55.301[4]).

Knowingly Violating Notary Public Act in Real Estate Transaction. Effective January 1, 2012, Senate Bill 252 and House Bill 4492 amend MCL 55.309, making it a felony to knowingly violate the Notary Public Act when notarizing a document relating to an interest in real property or a mortgage transaction. A conviction could result in a fine of up to $5,000, four years imprisonment or both,

Mortgage Fraud. On October 20, 2011, the Governor signed several recent bills to address the growing problem of mortgage and real property fraud. The first, effective immediately upon the Governor's signing, was Senate Bill 251 which put into place a 10-year statute of limitations to secure indictments for false pretenses involving real property, mortgage fraud, forgery or uttering and publishing an instrument affecting an interest in real property.

Also effective January 1, 2012, House Bill 4462 further addresses real property fraud, particularly those who falsely make, alter, or counterfeit a deed, discharge of mortgage or power of attorney affecting an interest in real property with intent to injure or defraud a person. A person found guilty of those or of publishing as true a false, forged, altered or counterfeit deed, discharge of mortgage or power of attorney is guilty of a felony punishable by imprisonment for not more than 14 years.

Finally, effective January 1, 2012, Senate Bill 43 enacted the state's first comprehensive mortgage fraud statute. The bill defines "mortgage lending process" as the process through which a person seeks or obtains a residential mortgage loan, including solicitation, application, or origination, negotiation of terms, third-party provider services, underwriting, signing and closing, and funding of the loan. Documents involved in the mortgage lending process include both mortgages and deeds, both routinely acknowledged before Notaries.

Significantly, the new law defines as a person who commits mortgage fraud any individual or corporation, limited liability company, partnership, trustee, association, or other legal entity. An employer of any person who commits mortgage fraud — including a Notary — could be liable to the criminal penalties provided in the new law.

Misdemeanor

A person committing violations of the Michigan Notary Public Act for which penalties are not other wise prescribed may be guilty of a misdemeanor punishable by a fine of not more than $5,000 or by imprisonment for not more than 1 year or both (MCL 55.309[1]). ■

Test Your Knowledge

Trial Exam

Instructions. This examination is designed to test your knowledge of the basic concepts of notarization. Although the state of Michigan does not require prospective Notaries to pass an exam before granting a commission, this Primer and any other instructional materials provided by the Michigan Department of State should be studied thoroughly to become familiar with notarial acts and duties.

Work through this exam without looking at the answers, then check your responses and note where you need additional study. Careful review of "Notary Laws Explained" (pages 19–65), the Michigan Notary statutes (pages 71–92), "10 Most-Asked Questions" (pages 9–13) and "Steps to Proper Notarization" (pages 14–18) will produce the answers.

A perfect score on this examination is 100 points. There are:

- 20 true/false questions worth 1 point each
- 5 multiple-choice questions worth 4 points each
- 5 fill-in-the-blank questions worth 4 points each
- 5 essay questions worth 8 points each.

Now, get a separate sheet of paper and a pen or pencil, and get ready to test your knowledge.

Part 1: True/False. For the following statements, answer true or false. Each correct answer is worth 1 point:

1. Notaries may act only in the county where they are commissioned. True or false?

2. The maximum Notary fee for taking an acknowledgment is $10. True or false?

3. Oaths and affirmations have the same legal effect. True or false?

4. Protests are one of the most common forms of notarization. True or false?

5. Notaries are obligated to ensure the truthfulness of the statements in the documents they notarize. True or false?

6. It is the duty of the Notary to decide on the type of notarization that is appropriate for a given document. True or false?

7. Though not legally required in Michigan, use of a Notary seal and journal is a good practice. True or false?

8. A subscribing witness must sign the document in addition to the principal signer. True or false?

9. An employee of a corporation may administer oaths to other officers and stockholders of that corporation. True or false?

10. Notaries may use their own wills as models in advising clients about how to handle their estates. True or false?

11. An affidavit requiring a jurat must be signed in the Notary's presence. True or false?

12. An acknowledged document, such as a deed, must be signed in the Notary's presence. True or false?

13. A Social Security card and a birth certificate offer reliable proof of a document signer's identity. True or false?

14. An affiant must do more than merely nod in assent to an oath. True or false?

15. The letters "S.S." indicate that Notaries must write in their Social Security numbers. True or false?

16. Certifying a copy is not an official notarial act in Michigan. True or false?

17. It is illegal to notarize a document whose blank spaces will be filled in later. True or false?

18. On a notarial certificate, the venue indicates where the Notary's oath has been filed. True or false?

19. Although technically different, the terms "affiant" and "deponent" are sometimes interchanged. True or false?

20. Notaries may notarize their own signatures. True or false?

Multiple Choice. Choose the one best answer to each question. Each correct answer is worth 4 points.

1. In executing an acknowledgment, a Notary certifies that …
   a. The signer took an oath or affirmation.
   b. The signer was positively identified by the Notary.
   c. The signer signed in the Notary's presence.

2. In executing a jurat, a Notary certifies that …
   a. The signer is of legal age.
   b. The signer signed in the Notary's presence.
   c. The signer has no direct interest in the document.

3. A certificate of authentication may be obtained …
   a. From the governor's office or the county clerk.
   b. From a stationery store or directly from the Notary.
   c. From the Department of State or the county clerk.

4. Notaries may be liable …
   a. Only for their intentional acts.
   b. Only for damages suffered by the signer.
   c. For all damages caused by their misconduct.

5. It could be the unauthorized practice of law to …
   a. Explain a paragraph in an immigration document.
   b. Provide a notarial certificate requested by the signer.
   c. Type a paper following the signer's instructions.

Fill in the Blank. Write in the word or phrase that best completes each sentence. Each correct answer is worth 4 points.

1. A ____________ must sometimes be attached to a notarized document sent out of state.

2. An affirmation is a solemn, spoken pledge that does not refer to a ____________.

3. The best ID cards contain the following three elements: a) ____________; b) ____________; and c)____________.

4. Without ID cards or personal knowledge of a signer's identity, Notaries may rely on the oath of a ____________ to identify the stranger.

5. The state official who appoints and regulates Notaries is the ____________.

Essay. Reply to each question or statement with a short paragraph. Each complete and correct response is worth 8 points.

1. Under what conditions should a Notary execute a protest?

2. Why do most Notaries never execute depositions?

3. Why is a Social Security card all but worthless as an ID?

4. May Notaries notarize for relatives?

5. Outline the differences between an acknowledgment certificate and a jurat.

Test Answers

True/False. 1. F; 2. T; 3 T; 4. F; 5 F; 6. F; 7. T; 8. T; 9. T; 10. F; 11. T; 12. F; 13. F; 14. T; 15. F; 16. T; 17. F; 18. F; 19. T; 20. F

Multiple Choice. 1. b; 2. b; 3. c; 4. c; 5. a

Fill In The Blank. 1. certificate of authentication; 2. Supreme Being; 3. photograph, signature and physical description; 4. credible identifying witness; 5. Secretary of State

Essay. Responses should include the basic information in the paragraphs below:

1. Because Michigan Notary law does not expressly authorize Notaries to execute protests, persons requesting this act should be referred to an experienced bank officer or an attorney familiar with the Uniform Commercial Code.

2. Depositions are normally executed by professional shorthand reporters who are able to readily transcribe oral testimony.

3. A Social Security card is very easily counterfeited and has only one of the three vital elements of a good ID: a signature. Reliable IDs also bear a photograph and a physical description.

4. No. Michigan Notaries are prohibited by law from notarizing for a lineal ancestor including parents and grandparents by state law. Notarizing for other family members, especially parents, violates restrictions against notarizing with a financial interest. Notaries should fully live up to their roles as impartial witnesses and never notarize for close relatives.

5. An acknowledgment certificate certifies that the signer of the document personally appeared before the Notary on the date and in the county indicated. It also certifies that the signer's identity was satisfactorily proven to the Notary and that the signer acknowledged having signed freely. A jurat certifies that the person signing the document signed in the Notary's presence, that the signer personally appeared before the Notary on the date and in the county indicated, was identified by the Notary and that an oath or affirmation was administered to the signer by the Notary.

Tally Your Score

After checking your answers, add up your score. Then look at the grading scale below to determine how you stand:

- 90–100: Excellent!
- 80–89: Good, but some review needed.
- 70–79: Fair. Reread the parts of the Primer covering the answers you missed.
- Below 70: Below par. Study the laws thoroughly again. ■

Michigan Laws Pertaining to Notaries Public

Reprinted on the following pages are pertinent sections of Michigan statutes affecting Notaries and notarial acts, mostly drawn from the Michigan Compiled Laws.

MICHIGAN STATUTES

MICHIGAN COMPILED LAWS

55.261. This act shall be known and may be cited as the "Michigan notary public act".

55.263. As used in this act:

(a) "Acknowledgment" means the confirmation by a person in the presence of a notary public that he or she is placing or has placed his or her signature on a record for the purposes stated in the record and, if the record is signed in a representative capacity, that he or she is placing or has placed his or her signature on the record with the proper authority and in the capacity of the person represented and identified in the record.

(b) "Cancellation" means the nullification of a notary public commission due to an error or defect or because the notary public is no longer entitled to the commission.

(c) "Department" means the department of state.

(d) "Electronic" means that term as defined in the uniform electronic transactions act, 2000 PA 305, MCL 450.831 to 450.849.

(e) "Electronic signature in global and national commerce act" means Public Law 106-229, 114 Stat. 464.

(f) "Information" means that term as defined in the electronic signature in global and national commerce act.

(g) "In a representative capacity" means any of the following:

(i) For and on behalf of a corporation, partnership, trust, association, or other legal entity as an authorized officer, agent, partner, trustee, or other representative of the entity.

(ii) As a public officer, personal representative, guardian, or other representative in the capacity recited in the document.

(iii) As an attorney in fact for a principal.

(iv) In any other capacity as an authorized representative of another person.

(h) "In the presence of" means in compliance with section 101(g) of title I of the electronic signature in global and national commerce act, 15 USC 7001.

55.265. As used in this act:

(a) "Jurat" means a certification by a notary public that a signer, whose identity is personally known to the notary public or proven on the basis of satisfactory evidence, has made in the presence of the notary public a voluntary signature and taken an oath or affirmation vouching for the truthfulness of the signed record.

(b) "Lineal ancestor" means an individual in the direct line of ascent including, but not limited to, a parent or grandparent.

(c) "Lineal descendant" means an individual in the direct line of descent including, but not limited to, a child or grandchild.

(d) "Notarial act" means any act that a notary public commissioned in this state is authorized to perform including, but not limited to, the taking of an acknowledgment, the administration of an oath or affirmation, the taking of a verification upon oath or affirmation, and the witnessing or attesting a signature performed in compliance with this act and the uniform recognition of acknowledgments act, 1969 PA 57, MCL 565.261 to 565.270.

(e) "Notify" means to communicate or send a message by a recognized mail, delivery service, or electronic means.

(f) "Official misconduct" means either or both of the following:

(i) The exercise of power or the performance of a duty that is unauthorized, unlawful, abusive, negligent, reckless, or injurious.

(ii) The charging of a fee that exceeds the maximum amount authorized by law.

(g) "Person" means every natural person, corporation, partnership, trust, association, or other legal entity and its legal successors.

(h) "Record" means that term as defined in the uniform electronic transactions act, 2000 PA 305, MCL 450.831 to 450.849.

(i) "Revocation" means the termination of a notary public's commission.

55.267. As used in this act:

(a) "Secretary" means the secretary of state acting directly or through his or her duly authorized deputies, assistants, and employees.

(b) "Signature" means a person's written or printed name or electronic signature as that term is defined in the uniform electronic transactions act, 2000 PA 305, MCL 450.831 to 450.849, or the person's mark attached to or logically associated with a record including, but not limited to, a contract and executed or adopted by the person with the intent to sign the record.

(c) "Suspension" means the temporary withdrawal of the notary's commission to perform notarial acts during the period of the suspension.

(d) "Verification upon oath or affirmation" means the declaration by oath or affirmation that a statement is true.

55.269. (1) The secretary may appoint as a notary public a person who complies with the requirements of this act.

(2) A notary public may reside in, move to, and perform notarial acts anywhere in this state from the date of appointment until the notary's birthday occurring not less than 6 years and not more than 7 years after the date of his or her appointment unless the appointment is canceled, suspended, or revoked by the secretary or by operation of law.

(3) The secretary shall not appoint as a notary public a person who is serving a term of imprisonment in a state correctional facility or jail in this or any other state or in a federal correctional facility.

55.271. (1) The secretary may appoint as a notary public a person who applies to the secretary and meets all of the following qualifications:

(a) Is at least 18 years of age.

(b) Is a resident of this state or maintains a principal place of business in this state.

(c) Reads and writes in the English language.

(d) Is free of any felony convictions, misdemeanor convictions, and violations as described in section 41.

(e) For a person who does not reside in the state of Michigan, demonstrates that his or her principal place of business is located in the county in which he or she requests appointment and indicates that he or she is engaged in an activity in which he or she is likely to be required to perform notarial acts as that word is defined in section 2 of the uniform recognition of acknowledgments act, 1969 PA 57, MCL 565.262.

(f) If applicable, has filed with the county clerk of his or her county of residence or expected appointment a proper surety bond and an oath taken as prescribed by the constitution in a format acceptable to the secretary. The requirement of filing a bond does not apply to an applicant that demonstrates, in a manner acceptable to the secretary, licensure as an attorney at law in this state.

(2) The secretary shall, on a monthly basis, notify the county clerk's office of the appointment of any notaries.

55.273. (1) Within 90 days before filing an application for a notary public appointment, a person shall file with the county clerk of his or her residence or expected appointment a proper surety bond and an oath taken as prescribed by the constitution.

(2) The bond shall be in the sum of $10,000.00 with good and sufficient surety by a surety licensed to do business in this state. The bond shall be conditioned upon indemnifying or reimbursing a person, financing agency, or governmental agency for monetary loss caused through the official misconduct of the notary public in the performance of a notarial act. The surety is required to indemnify or reimburse only after a judgment based on official misconduct has been entered in a court of competent jurisdiction against the notary public. The aggregate liability of the surety shall not exceed the sum of the bond. The surety on the bond may cancel the bond 60 days after the surety notifies the notary, the secretary and the county clerk of the cancellation. The surety is not liable for a breach of a condition occurring after the effective date of the cancellation. The county clerk shall not accept the personal assets of an applicant as security for a surety bond under this act.

(3) Each person who files an oath and, if applicable, a bond with a county clerk as required in subsection (1) shall pay a $10.00 filing fee to the county clerk. Upon receipt of the filing fee, the county clerk shall give a bond and oath certificate of filing to the person as prescribed by the secretary. A charter county with a population of more than 2,000,000 may impose by ordinance a fee for the county clerk's services different than the amount prescribed by this subsection. Two dollars of each fee collected under this subsection shall be deposited into the notary education and training fund established in section 17 on a schedule determined by the secretary.

55.275. (1) A person shall apply to the secretary for appointment as a notary public in a format as prescribed by the secretary. An application for appointment as a notary public shall contain the signature of the applicant. In addition to other information as may be required by the secretary, the application shall include all of the following:

(a) The applicant's name, residence address, business address, date of birth, and residence and business telephone numbers.

(b) The applicant's driver license or state personal identification card number.

(c) A validated copy of the filing of the bond, if applicable, and oath certificate of filing received from the county clerk.

(d) If applicable, a statement showing whether the applicant has previously applied for an appointment as a notary public in this or any other state, the result of the application, and whether the applicant has ever been the holder of a notary public appointment that was revoked, suspended, or canceled in this or any other state.

(e) A statement describing the date and circumstances of any felony or other misdemeanor conviction of the applicant during the preceding 10 years.

(f) A declaration that the applicant is a citizen of the United States or, if not a citizen of the United States, proof of the applicant's legal presence in this country.

(g) An affirmation by the applicant that the application is correct, that the applicant has read this act, and that the applicant will perform his or her notarial acts faithfully.

(2) Each application shall be accompanied by an application processing fee of $10.00. One dollar of each fee collected under this subsection shall be deposited into the notary education and training fund established in section 17 on a schedule determined by the secretary.

(3) Upon receipt of an application that is accompanied by the prescribed processing fee, the secretary may inquire as to the qualifications of the applicant and shall determine whether the applicant meets the qualifications prescribed in this act. To assist in deciding whether the applicant is qualified, the secretary may use the law enforcement information network as provided in the C.J.I.S. policy council act 1974 PA 163, MCL 28.211 to 28.215, to check the criminal background of the applicant.

(4) After approval of the application, the secretary shall mail directly to the applicant the certificate of appointment as a notary public. Each certificate of appointment shall identify the person as a notary public of this state and shall specify the term and country of the person's commission.

55.277. (1) The notary education and training fund is created within the state treasury. Money from fees collected under sections 13(3), 15(2), and 21(4) shall be deposited into the fund.

(2) The state treasurer may receive money or other assets from any source for deposit into the fund. The state treasurer shall direct the investment of the fund. The state treasurer shall credit to the fund interest and earnings from fund investments.

(3) Up to $150,000.00 shall remain in the fund at the close of each fiscal year and shall not lapse to the general fund. Any amount in excess of $150,000.00 shall lapse to the general fund.

(4) The secretary shall expend money from the fund in the form of grants, upon appropriation, for the purposes of providing education and training programs for county clerks and their staffs including, but not limited to, notary responsibilities, election worker training, and election processes. The secretary shall consult with the president of the Michigan association of county clerks, or his or her designee, when approving grant applications under this section.

(5) The secretary shall annually file a report regarding the balance of the fund at the time of the report and a detailed account of the expenditures in the preceding fiscal year. This report shall be sent to the speaker of the house of representatives, the minority leader of the house of representatives, the majority leader of the senate, and the minority leader of the senate.

55.279. (1) The secretary shall not automatically reappoint a notary public.

(2) A person desiring another notary public appointment may apply to the secretary, in a format prescribed by the secretary, for an original appointment as a notary public. The application may be submitted not more than 60 days before the expiration of his or her current notary public commission.

(3) In the case of a licensed attorney granted an appointment as a notary public under this Act and after the initial application under section 15, the secretary shall send a reappointment application form to the licensed attorney at least 90 days before the expiration of the current Notary appointment. The application for reappointment shall contain a certification to be completed by the applicant certifying that he or she is still a member in good standing in the state bar of Michigan. The applicant shall otherwise comply with the requirements for appointment as a notary public as described in section 15.

(4) The secretary shall automatically cancel the notary public commission of any person who makes, draws, utters, or delivers any check, draft, or order for the payment of a processing fee under this act that is not honored by the bank, financial institution, or other depository expected to pay the check, draft, or order for payment upon its first presentation.

55.281. (1) A notary public shall immediately apply to the secretary, in a format prescribed by the secretary, for a corrected notary public commission upon the occurrence of any of the following circumstances:

(a) A change in the notary public's name.

(b) A change in the notary public's residence or business address.

(c) The issuance by the secretary of a notary public commission that contains an error in the person's name, birth date, county, or other pertinent information if the error was made on the notary public's application and was used by the secretary to appoint the person as a notary public.

(2) A notary public shall immediately notify both the secretary and the county clerk of his or her appointment, in a format prescribed by the secretary, upon any change in the factual information stated in the notary public's application for appointment.

(3) The secretary shall notify the county clerk of the applicant's appointment when a corrected commission is issued by the secretary.

(4) If a notary public's certificate of appointment becomes lost, mutilated, or illegible, the notary public shall promptly apply to the secretary for the issuance of a duplicate certificate. The application shall be made on a form prescribed by the secretary and be accompanied by a processing fee of $10.00. One dollar of each processing fee collected under this subsection shall be deposited into the notary education and training fund established in section 17.

55.283. Before a notary public performs any notarial act, the notary public shall obtain and read a copy of all the current statutes of this state that regulate notarial acts.

55.285. (1) A notary public may perform notarial acts that include, but are not limited to, the following:

(a) Taking acknowledgments.

(b) Administering oaths and affirmations.

(c) Witnessing or attesting to a signature.

(2) In taking an acknowledgment, the notary public shall determine, either from personal knowledge or from satisfactory evidence, that the person in the presence of the notary public and making the acknowledgment is the person whose signature is on the record.

(3) In taking a verification upon oath or affirmation, the notary public shall determine, either from personal knowledge or from satisfactory evidence, that the person in the presence of the notary public and making the verification is the person whose signature is on the record being verified.

(4) In witnessing or attesting to a signature, the notary public shall determine, either from personal knowledge or from satisfactory evidence, that the signature is that of the person in the presence of the notary public and is the person named in the record.

(5) In all matters where the notary public takes a verification upon oath or affirmation, or witnesses or attests to a signature, the notary public shall require that the person sign the record being verified, witnessed, or attested in the presence of the notary public.

(6) A notary public has satisfactory evidence that a person is the person whose signature is on a record if that person is any of the following:

(a) Personally known to the notary public.

(b) Identified upon the oath or affirmation of a credible witness personally known by the notary public and who personally knows the person.

(c) Identified on the basis of a current license, identification card, or record issued by a federal or state government that contains the person's photograph and signature.

(7) The fee charged by a notary public for performing a notarial act

shall not be more than $10.00 for any individual transaction or notarial act. A notary public shall either conspicuously display a sign or expressly advise a person concerning the fee amount to be charged for a notarial act before the notary public performs the act. Before the notary public commences to travel in order to perform a notarial act, the notary public and client may agree concerning a separate travel fee to be charged by the notary public for traveling to perform the notarial act.

(8) A notary public may refuse to perform a notarial act.

(9) The secretary shall prescribe the form that a notary public shall use for a jurat, the taking of an acknowledgment, the administering of an oath or affirmation, the taking of a verification upon an oath or affirmation, the witnessing or attesting to a signature, or any other act that a notary public is authorized to perform in this state.

(10) A county clerk may collect a processing fee of $10.00 for certifying a notarial act of a notary public.

55.287. (1) A notary public shall place his or her signature on every record upon which he or she performs a notarial act. The notary public shall sign his or her name exactly as his or her name appears on his or her application for commission as a notary public.

(2) On each record that a notary public performs a notarial act and immediately near the notary public's signature, as is practical, the notary public shall print, type, stamp, or otherwise imprint mechanically or electronically sufficiently clear and legible to be read by the secretary and in a manner capable of photographic reproduction all of the following in this format or in a similar format that conveys all of the same information:

(a) The name of the notary public exactly as it appears on his or her application for commission as a notary public.

(b) The statement: "Notary public, State of Michigan, County of ________."

(c) The statement: "My commission expires ________________.".

(d) If performing a notarial act in a county other than the county of commission, the statement: "Acting in the County of ________________.".

(e) The date the notarial act was performed.

(3) A notary public may use a stamp seal or electronic process that contains all of the information required by subsection (2). However, the stamp, seal, or electronic process shall not be used in a manner that renders anything illegible on the record being notarized. An embosser alone or any other method that cannot be reproduced shall not be used.

(4) The illegibility of the statements required in subsection (2) does not affect the validity of the transaction or record that was notarized.

55.289. Repealed.

55.291. (1) A notary public shall not certify or notarize that a record is either of the following:

(a) An original.

(b) A true copy of another record.

(2) A notary public shall not do any of the following:

(a) Perform a notarial act upon any record executed by himself or herself.

(b) Notarize his or her own signature.

(c) Take his or her own deposition or affidavit.

(3) A notary public shall not claim to have powers, qualifications, rights, or privileges that the office of notary does not provide, including the power to counsel on immigration matters.

(4) A notary public shall not, in any document, advertisement, stationery, letterhead, business card, or other comparable written material describing the role of the notary public, literally translate from English into another language terms or titles including, but not limited to, notary public, notary, licensed, attorney, lawyer, or any other term that implies the person is an attorney.

(5) A notary public who is not a licensed attorney and who advertises notarial services in a language other than English shall include in the document, advertisement, stationery, letterhead, business card, or other comparable written material the following, prominently displayed in the same language:

(a) The statement: "I am not an attorney and have no authority to give advice on immigration or other legal matters".

(b) The fees for notarial acts as specified by statute.

(6) A notary public may not use the term "notario publico" or any equivalent non-English term in any business card, advertisement, notice, or sign.

(7) A notary public shall not perform any notarial act in connection with a transaction if the notary public has a conflict of interest. As used in this subsection, "conflict of interest" means either or both of the following:

(a) The notary public has a direct financial or beneficial interest, other than the notary public fee, in the transaction.

(b) The notary public is named, individually, as a grantor, grantee, mortgagor, mortgagee, trustor, trustee, beneficiary, vendor, vendee, lessor, or lessee or as a party in some other capacity to the transaction.

(8) A notary public shall not perform a notarial act for a spouse, descendant, or sibling including in-laws, steps, or half-relatives.

(9) A notary public who is a stockholder, director, officer, or employee of a bank or other corporation may take the acknowledgment of a party to a record executed to or by the corporation, or to administer an oath to any other stockholder, director, officer, employee, or agent of the corporation. A notary public shall not take the acknowledgment of a record by or to a bank or other corporation of which he or she is a stockholder, director, officer, or employee, under circumstances where the notary public is named as a party to the record, either individually or as a representative of the bank or other corporation and the notary public is individually a party to the record.

(10) For purposes of subsection (7), a notary public has no direct financial or beneficial interest in a transaction where the notary public acts in the capacity of an agent, employee, insurer, attorney, escrow, or lender for a person having a direct financial or beneficial interest in the transaction.

55.293. A notary public may sign the name of a person whose physical characteristics limit his or her capacity to sign or make a mark on a record presented for notarization under all of the following conditions:

(a) The notary public is orally, verbally, physically, or through electronic or mechanical means provided by the person and directed by that person to sign that person's name.

(b) The person is in the physical presence of the notary public.

(c) The notary public inscribes beneath the signature:

"Signature affixed pursuant to section 33 of the Michigan notary public act."

55.295. (1) Upon receiving a written or electronic request from the secretary, a notary public shall do all of the following as applicable:

(a) Furnish the secretary with a copy of the notary public's records that relate to the request.

(b) Within 15 days after receiving the request, respond to the secretary with information that relates to the official acts performed by the notary public.

(c) Permit the secretary to inspect his or her notary public records, contracts, or other information that pertains to the official acts of a notary public if those records, contracts, or other information is maintained by the notary public.

(2) Upon presentation to the secretary of satisfactory evidence that a notary public has failed to respond within 15 days or another time period designated under this act to a request of the secretary under subsection (1), the secretary may notify the notary public that his or her notary public commission is suspended indefinitely until he or she provides a satisfactory response to the request.

55.297. (1) For the official misconduct of a notary public, the notary public and the sureties on the notary public's surety bond are liable in a civil action for the damages sustained by the persons injured. The employer of a notary public is also liable if both of the following conditions apply:

(a) The notary public was acting within the actual or apparent scope of his or her employment.

(b) The employer had knowledge of and consented to or permitted the official misconduct.

(2) A notary public and the notary public's sureties are not liable for the truth, form, or correctness of the contents of a record upon which the notary public performs a notarial act.

55.299. The secretary may investigate, or cause to be investigated by local authorities, the administration of notary public laws and shall report violations of the notary public laws and rules to the attorney general or prosecuting attorney, or both, for prosecution.

55.300. (1) The secretary may, on his or her own initiative or in response to a complaint, make a reasonable and necessary investigation within or outside of this state and gather evidence concerning a person who violated, allegedly violated, or is about to violate this act, a rule promulgated under this act, or an order issued under this act or concerning whether a notary public is in compliance with this act, a rule promulgated under this act, or an order issued under this act.

(2) A person may file a complaint against a notary public with the secretary. A complaint shall be made in a format prescribed by the secretary and contain all of the following:

(a) The complainant's name, address, and telephone number.

(b) The complainant's signature and the date the complaint was signed.

(c) A complete statement describing the basis for the complaint.

(d) The actual record that is the basis for the complaint or a copy, photocopy, or other replica of the record.

(3) The secretary may investigate compliance with this act, the rules promulgated under it, or an order issued under it by examination of a notary public's records, contracts, and other pertinent records or information that relate to the official acts of the notary public.

55.300a. (1) An applicant for an appointment or a commissioned notary public who has engaged in conduct prohibited by this act, a rule promulgated under this act, or an order issued under this act is subject to 1 or more of the following penalties, in addition to any criminal penalties otherwise imposed:

(a) Suspension or revocation of his or her certificate of appointment.

(b) Denial of an application for appointment.

(c) A civil fine paid to the department in an amount not to exceed $1,000.00.

(d) A requirement to take the affirmative action determined necessary by the secretary, including payment of restitution to an injured person.

(e) A letter of censure.

(f) A requirement to reimburse the secretary for the costs of the investigation.

(2) The secretary may impose 1 or more of the penalties listed in subsection (1) upon presentation to the secretary of satisfactory evidence that the applicant for an appointment or a commissioned notary public has done 1 or more of the following:

(a) Violated this act, a rule promulgated under this act, or an order issued under this act or assisted others in the violation of this act, a rule promulgated under this act, or an order issued under this act.

(b) Committed an act of official misconduct, dishonesty, fraud, deceit, or of any cause substantially relating to the duties or responsibilities of a notary public or the character or public trust necessary to be a notary public.

(c) Failed to perform his or her notary public duties in accordance with this act, a rule promulgated under this act, or an order issued under this act.

(d) Failed to fully and faithfully discharge a duty or responsibility required of a notary public.

(e) Been found liable in a court of competent jurisdiction for damages in an action grounded in fraud, misrepresentation, or violation of this act.

(f) Represented, implied, or used false or misleading advertising that he or she has duties, rights, or privileges that he or she does not possess by law.

(g) Charged a fee for a notarial act that was more than is allowed under this act.

(h) Failed to complete the notary public's acknowledgment at the time the notary public signed or affixed his or her signature or seal to a record.

(i) Failed to administer an oath or affirmation as required by law.

(j) Engaged in the unauthorized practice of law as determined by a court of competent jurisdiction.

(k) Ceased to maintain his or her residence or principal place of business in this state.

(l) Lacks adequate ability to read and write English.

(m) Hindered or refused a request by the secretary for notary public records or papers.

(n) Engaged in a method, act, or practice that is unfair or deceptive including the making of an untrue statement of a material fact relating to a duty or responsibility of a notary public.

(o) Violated a condition of probation imposed under subsection (1).

(p) Permitted an unlawful use of a notary public's seal.

(q) Failed to maintain good moral character as defined and determined under 1974 PA 381, MCL 338.41 to 338.47.

(3) Before the secretary takes any action under subsection (2), the person affected shall be given notice and an opportunity for a hearing.

(4) If a person holding office as a notary public is sentenced to a term of imprisonment in a state correctional facility or jail in this or any other state or in a federal correctional facility, that person's commission as a notary public is revoked automatically on the day on which the person begins serving the sentence in the jail or correctional facility. If a person's commission as a notary public is revoked because the person begins serving a term of imprisonment and that person performs or attempts to perform a notarial act while imprisoned, that person is not eligible to receive a commission as a notary public for at least 10 years after the person completes his or her term of imprisonment.

(5) Cancellation of a commission is without prejudice to reapplication at any time. A person whose commission is revoked is ineligible for the issuance of a new commission for at least 5 years.

(6) A fine imposed under this act that remains unpaid for more than 180 days may be referred to the department of treasury for collection. The department of treasury may collect the fine by deducting the amount owed from a payroll or tax refund warrant. The secretary may bring an action in a court of competent jurisdiction to recover the amount of a civil fine.

55.301. (1) If a notary public of this state is convicted of a felony or of a substantially corresponding violation of another state, the secretary shall automatically revoke the notary public commission of that person on the date that the person's felony conviction is entered.

(2) If a notary public of this state is convicted of 2 or more misdemeanor offenses involving a violation of this act within a 12-month period while commissioned, or of 3 or more misdemeanor offenses involving a violation of this act within a 5-year period regardless of being commissioned, the secretary shall automatically revoke the notary public commission of that person on the date that the person's most recent misdemeanor conviction is entered.

(3) If a person holding office as a notary public is sentenced to a term of imprisonment in a state correctional facility or jail in this or any other state or in a federal correctional facility, that person's commission as a notary public is revoked automatically on the day on which the person begins serving the sentence in the jail or correctional facility. If a person's commission as a notary public is revoked because the person begins serving a term of imprisonment and that person performs or attempts to perform a notarial act while imprisoned, that person is not eligible to receive a commission as a notary public for at least 10 years after the

person completes his or her term of imprisonment.

(4) A person found guilty of performing a notarial act after his or her commission is revoked under this section is guilty of a felony punishable by a fine of not more than $3,000.00 or by imprisonment for not more than 5 years, or both.

(5) A person, regardless of whether he or she has ever been commissioned as a notary public, that is convicted of a felony is disqualified from being commissioned as a notary public for not less than 10 years after the person completes his or her sentence for that crime, including any term of imprisonment, parole, or probation, and pays all fines, costs, and assessments. As used in this section, a "felony" means a violation of a penal law of this state, another state, or the United States for which the offender, upon conviction, may be punished by death or imprisonment for more than 1 year or an offense expressly designated by law to be a felony.

(6) If a person is convicted of a violation described in subsection (5), the court shall make a determination of whether the person is a notary. If the person is a notary, the court shall inform the secretary of the conviction.

55.303. (1) Cancellation of a commission is without prejudice to reapplication at any time. Except as otherwise provided for in section 41(3), a person whose commission is revoked is ineligible for the issuance of a new commission for at least 5 years.

(2) A fine imposed under this act that remains unpaid for more than 180 days may be referred to the department of treasury for collection. The department of treasury may collect the fine by deducting the amount owed from a payroll or tax refund warrant. The secretary may bring an action in a court of competent jurisdiction to recover the amount of a civil fine.

55.305. (1) Whenever it appears to the secretary that a person has engaged or is about to engage in an act or practice that constitutes or will constitute a violation of this act, a rule promulgated under this act, or an order issued under this act, the attorney general may petition a circuit court for injunctive relief. Upon a proper showing, a circuit court may issue a permanent or temporary injunction or restraining order to enforce the provisions of this act. A party to the action has the right to appeal within 60 days from the date the order or judgment of the court was issued.

(2) The court may order a person subject to an injunction or restraining order provided for in this section to reimburse the secretary for the actual expenses incurred in the investigation related to the petition. The secretary shall refund any amount received as reimbursement should the injunction or restraining order later be dissolved by an appellate court.

55.307. (1) Subject to subsection (2) and in the courts of this state, the certificate of a notary public of official acts performed in the capacity of a notary public, under the seal of office, is presumptive evidence of the facts contained in the certificate except that the certificate is not evidence of a notice of nonacceptance or nonpayment in any case in which a defendant attaches to his or her pleadings an affidavit denying the fact of having received that notice of nonacceptance or nonpayment.

(2) Notwithstanding subsection (1), the court may invalidate any notarial act not performed in compliance with this act.

55.309. (1) Except as otherwise provided for in section 41(4) or as provided by law, a person who violates this act is guilty of 1 of the following:

(A) Except as provided in subdivision (B), a misdemeanor punishable by a fine of not more than $5,000.00 or by imprisonment for not more than 1 year, or both.

(B) If the person knowingly violates this act when notarizing any document relating to an interest in real property or a mortgage transaction, a felony punishable by a fine of not more than $5,000 or by imprisonment for not more than 4 years, or both.

(2) An action concerning a fee charged for a notarial act shall be filed in the district court in the place where the notarial act occurred.

(3) The penalties and remedies under this act are cumulative. The bringing of an action or prosecution under this act does not bar an action or prosecution under any other applicable law.

Enacting Section 1 of this amendatory act takes effect January 1, 2012.

55.311. (1) The notary fees fund is created in the state treasury. Except as otherwise provided in sections 15(2) and21(4), an application processing fee, duplicate notary public certificate of appointment service charge, certification processing fee, copying processing fee, reimbursement costs, or administrative fine collected under this act by the secretary shall be deposited by the state treasurer in the notary fees fund and is appropriated to defray the costs incurred by the secretary in administering this act.

(2) A processing or filing fee paid to the secretary or county clerk under this act is not refundable.

55.313. A person, or the personal representative of a person who is deceased, who both performed a notarial act and created a record of the act performed while commissioned as a notary public under this act shall maintain all the records of that notarial act for at least 5 years after the date of the notarial act.

55.315. The secretary may promulgate rules pursuant to the administrative procedures act of 1969, 1969 PA 306, MCL 24.201 to 24.328, to implement this act.

Enacting section 1. The following acts and parts of acts are repealed effective April 1, 2004:

(a) Executive Reorganization Order No. 1980-2, MCL 55.103.

(b) Sections 107, 108, 109, 110, 111, 112, 112a, 113, 114, 115, 116, and 117 of 1846 RS 14, MCL 55.107, 55.108, 55.109, 55.110, 55.111, 55.112, 55.112a, 55.113, 55.114, 55.115, 55.116, and 55.117.

(c) 1903 PA 18, MCL 55.221.

(d) 1909 PA 18, MCL 55.251.

(e) Section 2564 of the revised judicature act of 1961, 1961 PA 236, MCL 600.2564.

Enacting section 2. This act takes effect April 1, 2004.
This act is ordered to take immediate effect.

Clerk of the House of Representatives
Secretary of the Senate
Approved
Governor

OTHER PERTINENT STATUTES

565.261. Short title

Sec. 1. This act shall be known and may be cited as the "uniform recognition of acknowledgments act".

(1969 Public Act 57)

565.262. Notarial acts, definition; persons performing out of state

Sec. 2. (a) "Notarial acts" means acts that the laws of this state authorize notaries public of this state to perform, including the administering of oaths and affirmations, taking proof of execution and acknowledgments of instruments, and attesting documents. Notarial acts may be performed outside this state for use in this state with the same effect as if performed by a notary public of this state by the following persons authorized pursuant to the laws and regulations of other governments in addition to any other person authorized by the laws of this state:

(i) A notary public authorized to perform notarial acts in the place in which the act is performed.

(ii) A judge, clerk or deputy clerk of any court of record in the place in which the notarial acts are performed.

(iii) An officer of the foreign service of the United States, a consular agent or any other person authorized by regulation of the United States department of state to perform notarial acts in the place in which the act is performed.

(iv) A commissioned officer in active service with the armed forces of the United States and any other person authorized by regulation of the armed forces to perform notarial acts if the notarial acts are performed for 1 of the following or his or her dependents:

(A) A merchant seaman of the United States.

(B) A member of the armed forces of the United States.

(C) Any other person serving with or accompanying the armed forces of the United States.

(v) Any other person authorized to perform notarial acts in the place in which the act is performed.

(b) "Satisfactory evidence" means evidence upon which reliance is placed upon either of the following:

(i) The sworn word of a credible witness who is personally known to the notary public and who personally knows the signer.

(ii) A current identification card or document issued by a federal or state government that contains the bearer's photograph and signature.

(Amended, 1997 Public Act 5)

565.263. Authority of officer, authentication

Sec. 3. (1) If the notarial act is performed by any of the persons described in subdivisions (a) to (d) of section 2, other than a person authorized to perform notarial acts by the laws or regulations of a foreign country, the signature, rank or title and serial number, if any, of the person are sufficient proof of the authority of a holder of that rank or title to perform the act. Further proof of his authority is not required.

(2) If the notarial act is performed by a person authorized by the laws or regulations of a foreign country to perform the act, there is sufficient proof of the authority of that person to act if any of the following exist:

(a) Either a foreign service officer of the United States resident in the country in which the act is performed or a diplomatic or consular officer of the foreign country resident in the United States certifies that a person holding that office is authorized to perform the act.

(b) The official seal of the person performing the notarial act is affixed to the document.

(c) The title and indication of authority to perform notarial acts of the person appears either in a digest of foreign law or in a list customarily used as a source of such information.

(3) If the notarial act is performed by a person other than 1 described in subsections (1) and (2), there is sufficient proof of the authority of that person to act if the clerk of a court of record in the place in which the notarial act is performed certifies to the official character of that person and to his authority to perform the notarial act.

(4) The signature and title of the person performing the act are prima facie evidence that he is a person with the designated title and that the signature is genuine.

(1969 Public Act 57)

565.264. Certificate of person taking acknowledgment

Sec. 4. The person taking an acknowledgment shall certify that the person acknowledging appeared before him and acknowledged he executed the instrument; and the person acknowledging was known to the person taking the acknowledgment or that the person taking the acknowledgment had satisfactory evidence that the person acknowledging was the person described in and who executed the instrument.

(1969 Public Act 57)

565.265. Form of certificate of acknowledgment

Sec. 5. The form of a certificate of acknowledgment used by a person whose authority is recognized under section 2 shall be accepted in this state if 1 of the following is true:

(a) The certificate is in a form prescribed by the laws or regulations of this state.

(b) The certificate is in a form prescribed by the laws applicable in the place in which the acknowledgment is taken.

(c) The certificate contains the words "acknowledged before me", or their substantial equivalent.

(1969 Public Act 57)

565.266. Acknowledged before me, meaning

Sec. 6. The words "acknowledged before me" means:

(a) That the person acknowledging appeared before the person taking the acknowledgment.

(b) That he acknowledged he executed the instrument.

(c) That, in the case of:

(i) A natural person, he executed the instrument for the purposes therein stated.

(ii) A corporation, the officer or agent acknowledged he held the position or title set forth in the instrument and certificate, he signed the instrument on behalf of the corporation by proper authority and the instrument was the act of the corporation for the purposes therein stated.

(iii) A partnership, the partner or agent acknowledged he signed the instrument on behalf of the partnership by proper authority and he executed the instrument as the act of the partnership for the purposes therein stated.

(iv) A person acknowledging as principal by an attorney in fact, he executed the instrument by proper authority as the act of the principal for the purposes therein stated.

(v) A person acknowledging as a public officer, trustee, administrator, guardian or other representative, he signed the instrument by proper authority and he executed the instrument in the capacity and for the purposes therein stated.

(d) That the person taking the acknowledgment either knew or had satisfactory evidence that the person acknowledging was the person named in the instrument or certificate. (1969 Public Act 57)

565.267. Statutory short forms of acknowledgment

Sec. 7. (1) The forms of acknowledgment set forth in this section may be used and are sufficient for their purposes under any law of this state. The forms shall be known as "statutory short forms of acknowledgment" and may be referred to by that name. The authorization of the forms in this section does not preclude the use of other forms.

(2) For an individual acting in his own right:

State of ________
County of ________

The foregoing instrument was acknowledged before me this (date) by (name of person acknowledged).

(Signature of person taking acknowledgment)
(Title or rank)
(Serial number, if any)

(3) For a corporation:

State of ________
County of ________

The foregoing instrument was acknowledged before me this (date) by (name of officer or agent, title or [sic] officer or agent) of (name of corporation acknowledging) a (state or place of incorporation) corporation, on behalf of the corporation.

(Signature of person taking acknowledgment)
(Title or rank)
(Serial number, if any)
(4) For a partnership:

State of ________
County of ________

The foregoing instrument was acknowledged before me this (date) by (name of acknowledging partner or agent), partner (or agent) on behalf of (name of partnership), a partnership.
(Signature of person taking acknowledgment)
(Title or rank)
(Serial number, if any)

(5) For an individual acting as principal by an attorney in fact:

State of ________
County of ________

The foregoing instrument was acknowledged before me this (date) by (name of attorney in fact) as attorney in fact on behalf of (name of principal).
(Signature of person taking acknowledgment)
(Title or rank)
(Serial number, if any)

(6) By any public officer, trustee or personal representative:

State of ________
County of ________

The foregoing instrument was acknowledged before me this (date) by (name and title of position).

(Signature of person taking acknowledgment)
(Title or rank)
(Serial number, if any)

(1969 Public Act 57)

565.268. Prior notarial acts unaffected

Sec. 8. A notarial act performed prior to the effective date of this act is not affected by this act. This act provides an additional method of proving notarial acts. Nothing in this act diminishes or invalidates the recognition accorded to notarial acts by other laws of this state. (1969 Public Act 57)

565.269. Uniform interpretation

Sec. 9. This act shall be so interpreted as to make uniform the laws of those states which enact it.

(1969 Public Act 57)

565.270. Repealer

Sec. 10. Act No. 185 of the Public Acts of 1895, being sections 565.251 to 565.256 of the Compiled Laws of 1948, is repealed. (1969 Public Act 57)

565.281. Acknowledgment by married woman

Sec. 1. That hereafter the acknowledgment of any married woman to a deed of conveyance or other instrument affecting real property, may be taken in the same manner as if she were sole.

(1877 Public Act 62)

600.2564. Fees of notaries public

Sec. 2564. Notaries public shall be entitled to the following fees, which are not taxable as costs:

(1) For drawing and copy of protest of the nonpayment of a promissory note or bill of exchange, or of the nonacceptance of such bill, 50 cents, in cases where by law, such protest is necessary, but in no other case.

(2) For drawing and copy of every other protest, 25 cents.

(3) For drawing, copy, and serving every notice of nonpayment of a note, or nonacceptance of a bill, 25 cents.

(4) For drawing any affidavit, or other paper or proceeding, for which provision is not herein made, 20 cents for each folio, and for copying the same, 6 cents for each folio.

(5) For taking the acknowledgment of deeds, and for other services authorized by law, the same fees as are allowed to other officers for similar services.

(1961 Public Act 236, § 2564)

Executive Reorganization Order 1980-2

55.103 Transfer of notary public functions to department of state.

WHEREAS, Section 107 of the Revised Statutes of 1846, as amended, being section 55.107 of the Compiled Laws of 1970, assigns certain functions with respect to notaries public to the Governor; and

WHEREAS, all or any portion of those functions may be delegated by Executive Order to the Department of State pursuant to Section 33, Act 380 of the Public Acts of 1965, being Section 16.133 of the Michigan Compiled Laws of 1970; and

WHEREAS, all ministerial and clerical duties and functions relative to processing applications for notaries public were transferred and delegated to the Department of State by Executive Order 1970-3 on February 9, 1970; and

WHEREAS, all remaining powers, duties and functions of the Governor with respect to notaries public, being those vested by Sections 55.107 through 55.117 inclusive, of the Michigan Compiled Laws of 1970, except the appointment authority of the Governor set forth in the first sentence of Section 55. 107, were transferred and delegated to the Department of State by Executive Order 1976-11 on November 2, 1976,

NOW, THEREFORE, I, WILLIAM G. MILLIKEN, Governor of the State of Michigan, pursuant to Section 33, Act 380 of the Public Acts of 1965, do hereby revoke Executive Order 1970-3 and Executive Order 1976-11.

I further hereby delegate to the Department of State all powers, duties, and functions of the Governor with respect to notaries public, being those vested by Sections 55.107 through 55.117 inclusive, of the Michigan Compiled Laws of 1970, reserving none of these powers, duties, and functions.

This delegation and transfer shall become effective August 15, 1980. (1980 E.R.O. 1980-2)

UNIFORM REAL PROPERTY ELECTRONIC RECORDING ACT

Act 123 of 2010

565.841 Short title.

Sec. 1.

This act shall be known and may be cited as the "uniform real property electronic recording act".

History: 2010,Act 123, Imd. Eff. July 19, 2010

565.842 Definitions.

Sec. 2.

As used in this act:

(a) "Commission" means the electronic recording commission created in section 5.

(b) "Document" means information that is inscribed on a tangible medium or that is stored in an electronic or other medium and is retrievable in perceivable form, and that is eligible to be recorded in the land records maintained by the county register of deeds.

(c) "Electronic" means relating to technology having electrical, digital, magnetic, wireless, optical, electromagnetic, or similar capabilities.

(d) "Electronic document" means a document that is received by the county register of deeds in an electronic form.

(e) "Electronic signature" means an electronic sound, symbol, or process attached to or logically associated with a document and executed or adopted by a person with the intent to sign the document.

(f) "Paper document" means a document that is received by the county register of deeds in a form that is not electronic.

(g) "Person" means an individual, corporation, business trust, estate, trust, partnership, limited liability company, association, joint venture, public corporation, government, or governmental subdivision, agency, or instrumentality, or any other legal or commercial entity.

History: 2010,Act 123, Imd. Eff. July 19, 2010

565.843 Electronic document or signature; satisfaction of recording requirement; acceptance by register of deeds not required.

Sec. 3.

(1) If a law requires as a condition for recording that a document be an original, be on paper or another tangible medium, or be in writing, the requirement is satisfied by an electronic document.

(2) If a law requires as a condition for recording that a document be signed, the requirement is satisfied by an electronic signature.

(3) A requirement that a document or a signature associated with a document be notarized, acknowledged, verified, witnessed, or made under oath is satisfied if the electronic signature of the person authorized to perform that act, and all other information required to be included, is attached to or logically associated with the document or signature. A physical or electronic image of a stamp, impression, or seal need not accompany an electronic signature.

(4) This section does not require that a register of deeds accept electronic documents for recording.

History: 2010,Act 123, Imd. Eff. July 19, 2010

565.844 Establishment of standards by electronic recording commission; powers of county register of deeds; acceptance of paper documents; placement of entries in index; electronic documents recorded before establishment of standards.

Sec. 4.

(1) A county register of deeds who implements any of the functions listed in subsection (2) shall do so in compliance with any standards established by the electronic recording commission.

(2) A county register of deeds may do any of the following:

(a) Receive, index, store, archive, and transmit electronic documents.

(b) Provide for access to, and for search and retrieval of, documents and information by electronic means.

(c) Convert paper documents accepted for recording into electronic form.

(d) Convert into electronic form information recorded before the county register of deeds began to record electronic documents.

(e) Accept electronically any fee or tax that the county register of deeds is authorized to collect.

(f) Agree with other officials of a state or a political subdivision of a state, or of the United States, on procedures or processes to facilitate the electronic satisfaction of prior approvals and conditions precedent to recording and the electronic payment of fees or taxes.

(3) A county register of deeds who accepts electronic documents

for recording shall continue to accept paper documents for recording as authorized by state law. The county register of deeds shall place entries for both types of documents in the same index.

(4) This act does not invalidate electronic documents recorded under this act, the uniform electronic transactions act, 2000 PA 305, MCL 450.831 to 450.849, or the federal electronic signatures in global and national commerce act, 15 USC 7001 to 7031, before the establishment of standards under this act by the electronic recording commission.

History: 2010,Act 123, Imd. Eff. July 19, 2010

565.845 Electronic recording commission; creation; membership; terms; vacancy; removal; meetings; quorum; business conducted at public meeting; writing subject to freedom of information act; compensation; establishment of standards.

Sec. 5.

(1) Effective January 1, 2011, an electronic recording commission is created within the department of technology, management, and budget. The commission consists of 8 members, as follows:

(a) The director of the department of technology, management, and budget or his or her designee, who shall be a nonvoting member.

(b) Seven members appointed by the governor, as follows:

(i) Four shall be county registers of deeds.

(ii) One shall be an individual who is engaged in the land title profession.

(iii) One shall be an individual who is engaged in the business of banking.

(iv) One shall be an individual who is an attorney licensed to practice law in this state and whose practice emphasizes real property matters.

(2) The appointed members of the commission shall serve for terms of 2 years or until a successor is appointed, whichever is later, except that of the members first appointed 3 shall serve for 1 year, 2 shall serve for 2 years, and 2 shall serve for 3 years.

(3) If a vacancy occurs on the commission, the governor shall make an appointment for the unexpired term in the same manner as the original appointment.

(4) The governor may remove an appointed member of the commission for incompetency, dereliction of duty, malfeasance, misfeasance, or nonfeasance in office, or any other good cause.

(5) The first meeting of the commission shall be called by the director of the department of technology, management, and budget. At the first meeting, the commission shall elect from among its members a chairperson and other officers as it considers necessary or appropriate. After the first meeting, the commission shall meet at least quarterly, or more frequently at the call of the chairperson or if requested by 5 or more members.

(6) A majority of the members of the commission constitute a quorum for the transaction of business at a meeting of the commission. A majority of the members present and serving are required for official action of the commission.

(7) The business that the commission may perform shall be conducted at a public meeting of the commission held in compliance with the open meetings act, 1976 PA 267, MCL 15.261 to 15.275.

(8) A writing prepared, owned, used, in the possession of, or retained by the commission in the performance of an official function is subject to the freedom of information act, 1976 PA 442, MCL 15.231 to 15.246.

(9) Members of the commission shall serve without compensation. However, members of the commission may be reimbursed for their actual and necessary expenses incurred in the performance of their official duties as members of the commission.

(10) The commission shall adopt standards to implement this act. To keep the standards and practices of county registers of deeds in this state in harmony with the standards and practices of offices of county registers of deeds in other jurisdictions that enact substantially this act, and to keep the technology used by county registers of deeds in this state compatible with technology used by offices of county registers of deeds in other jurisdictions that enact substantially this act, the commission, so far as is consistent with the purposes, policies, and provisions of this act, in adopting, amending, and repealing standards, shall consider all of the following:

(a) Standards and practices of other jurisdictions.

(b) The most recent standards promulgated by national standard-setting bodies, such as the property records industry association.

(c) The views of interested persons and governmental officials and entities.

(d) The needs of counties of varying size, population, and resources.

(e) Standards requiring adequate information security protection to ensure that electronic documents are accurate, authentic, adequately preserved, and resistant to tampering.

History: 2010,Act 123, Imd. Eff. July 19, 2010

565.846 Application and construction of act.

Sec. 6.

In applying and construing this uniform act, consideration must be given to the need to promote uniformity of the law with respect to its subject matter among states that enact it.

History: 2010,Act 123, Imd. Eff. July 19, 2010

565.847 Federal electronic signatures; limitation of act.

Sec. 7.

This act modifies, limits, and supersedes the federal electronic signatures in global and national commerce act, 15 USC 7001, et seq., but does not modify, limit, or supersede section 101(c) of that act, 15 USC 7001(c), or authorize electronic delivery of any of the notices described in section 103(b) of that act, 15 USC 7003(b).

History: 2010,Act 123, Imd. Eff. July 19, 2010 ■

Office of the Michigan Department of State

The following office of the Michigan Department of State provides application forms for Notary Public commissions. Inquiries, requests for applications and information regarding apostilles and certificates of authority may be directed to:

Michigan Department of State
Office of the Great Seal
7064 Crowner Blvd.
Lansing, MI 48918
Telephone: (517) 335-8656

In addition, there are many useful resources available at the state's official Web site, including links to legislative information, the Secretary of State's office and other state departments. You can access the state's home page at *www.michigan.gov/*.

The Secretary of State may be located on the Web at *www.michigan.gov/sos*. ■

County Clerks' Offices

Within 90 days before submitting an application for a Notary Public appointment, each applicant must take and file an oath of office and $10,000 bond with the county clerk in the county in which he or she resides or, in the case of an out-of-state resident, maintains a principal place of business.

At these same offices, certificates authenticating a local Notary's signature on documents to be sent out of state may be obtained. (See "Authentication," pages 54–57.)

For certified copies of marriage certificates, contact the office of the county clerk where the certificate was filed. For certified copies of birth and death certificates, contact the appropriate Bureau of Vital Statistics. (See the listing beginning on page 97.)

Alcona
P.O. Box 308
Harrisville, MI 48740
(989) 724-6807

Alger
101 Court St.
Munising, MI 49862
(906) 387-2076

Allegan
113 Chestnut St.
Allegan, MI 49010
(269) 673-0555

Alpena
720 W. Chisholm
Alpena, MI 49707
(989) 354-6559

Antrim
P.O. Box 520
Bellaire, MI 49615
(231) 533-6353

Arenac
120 N. Grove
Standish, MI 48658
(989) 846-4626

Baraga
16 N. Third St.
L'Anse, MI 48946
(906) 524-6183

Barry
220 W. State St.
Hastings, MI 49058
(269) 945-1285

Bay
515 Center Ave.
Bay City, MI 48708
(989) 895-4280

Benzie
P.O. Box 377
Beulah, MI 49617
(231) 882-7671

Berrien
811 Port St.
St. Joseph, MI 49085
(269) 983-7111

Branch
31 Division St.
Coldwater, MI 49036
(517) 279-4306

Calhoun
315 W. Green St.
Marshall, MI 49068
(269) 781-0730

Cass
120 N. Broadway
Cassopolis, MI 49031
(269) 445-4464

Charlevoix
203 Antrim St.
Charlevoix, MI 49720
(231) 547-7200

Cheboygan
P.O. Box 70
Cheboygan, MI 49721
(231) 627-8808

Chippewa
319 Court St.
Sault Ste. Marie, MI
49783
(906) 635-6300

Clare
255 W. Main St.
Harrison, MI 48625
(989) 539-7131

Clinton
100 E. State St.
St. Johns, MI 48879
(989) 224-5140

Crawford
200 W. Michigan
Grayling, MI 49738
(989) 344-3200

Delta
310 Ludington
Escanaba, MI 49829
(906) 789-5105

Dickinson
705 S. Stephenson
Iron Mountain, MI
49801
(906) 774-0988

Eaton
1045 Independence
Charlotte, MI 48813
(517) 543-7500

Emmet
200 Division St.
Petoskey, MI 49770
(231) 348-1744

Genesee
900 S. Saginaw St.
Flint, MI 48502
(810) 257-3282

Gladwin
401 W. Cedar
Gladwin, MI 48624
(517) 426-7351

Gogebic
200 N. Moore
Bessemer, MI 49911
(906) 663-4518

Grand Traverse
400 Broadman
Traverse City, MI 49684
(231) 922-4760

Gratiot
P.O. Box 437
Ithaca, MI 48847
(517) 875-5215

Hillsdale
29 N. Howell
Hillsdale, MI 49242
(517) 437-3391

Houghton
401 E. Houghton
Houghton, MI 49931
(906) 482-1150

Huron
County Building
Bad Axe, MI 48413
(989) 269-9942

Ingham
County Building
Mason, MI 48854
(517) 676-7201

Ionia
100 Main St.
Ionia, MI 48846
(616) 527-5322

Iosco
P.O. Box 838
Tawas City, MI 48764
(989) 362-3497

Iron
2 South 6th St.
Crystal Falls, MI 49920
(906) 875-3221

Isabella
200 N. Main
Mt. Pleasant, MI 48858
(517) 772-0911

Jackson
312 S. Jackson
Jackson, MI 49201
(517) 788-4268

Kalamazoo
201 W. Kalamazoo
Kalamazoo, MI 49007
(269) 383-8840

Kalkaska
605 N. Birch St.
Kalkaska, MI 49646
(231) 258-3300

Kent
300 Monroe NW
Grand Rapids, MI
49503
(616) 336-3550

Keweenaw
HC 1, Box 607
Eagle River, MI 49950
(906) 337-2229

Lake
County Building
Baldwin, MI 49304
(231) 745-2725

Lapeer
255 Clay St.
Lapeer, MI 48446
(810) 667-0356

Leelanau
County Building
Leland, MI 49654
(231) 256-9824

Lenawee
425 Main St.
Adrian, MI 49221
(517) 264-4599

Livingston
200 E. Grand River
Howell, MI 48843
(517) 546-0500

Luce
407 W. Harrie
Newberry, MI 49868
(906) 293-5521

Mackinac
100 N. Marley St.
St. Ignace, MI 49781
(906) 643-7300

Macomb
40 N. Main
Mt. Clemens, MI 48043
(586) 469-5120

Manistee
415 Third St.
Manistee, MI 49660
(231) 723-3331

Marquette
234 W. Baraga Ave.
Marquette, MI 49855
(906) 225-8330

Mason
304 E. Ludington
Ludington, MI 49431
(231) 843-8202

Mecosta
400 Elm St.
Big Rapids, MI 49307
(231) 592-0783

Menominee
839 10th Ave.
Menominee, MI 49858
(906) 863-9968

Midland
220 W. Ellsworth
Midland, MI 48640
(989) 832-6739

Missaukee
111 S. Canal
Lake City, MI 49651
(231) 839-4967

Monroe
106 E. First St.
Monroe, MI 48161
(734) 240-7020

Montcalm
P.O. Box 368
Stanton, MI 48888
(989) 831-7339

Montmorency
P.O. Box 789
Atlanta, MI 49709
(989) 785-8022

Muskegon
990 Terrace St.
Muskegon, MI 49442
(231) 724-6221

Newaygo
1087 Newell
White Cloud, MI 49349
(231) 689-7235

Oakland
1200 N. Telegraph
Pontiac, MI 48341
(810) 858-0581

Oceana
County Building
Hart, MI 49420
(231) 873-4328

Ogemaw
806 W. Houghton
West Branch, MI 48661
(517) 345-0215

Ontonagon
725 Greenland
Ontonagon, MI 49953
(906) 884-4255

Osceola
301 W. Upton
Reed City, MI 49677
(231) 832-6104

Oscoda
P.O. Box 399
Mio, MI 48647
(989) 826-1110

Otsego
225 W. Main
Gaylord, MI 49735
(989) 731-7500

Ottawa
414 Washington
Grand Haven, MI
49417
(616) 846-8310

Presque Isle
151 E. Huron Ave.
Rogers City, MI 49779
(989) 734-3288

Roscommon
County Building
Roscommon, MI 48853
(989) 275-5923

St. Clair
201 McMorran
Port Huron, MI 48060
(810) 985-2200

St. Joseph
125 W. Main St.
Centreville, MI 49032
(616) 467-5602

Saginaw
111 S. Michigan
Saginaw, MI 48602
(989) 790-5251

Sanilac
60 W. Sanilac
Sandusky, MI 48471
(810) 648-3212

Schoolcraft
300 Walnut
Manistique, MI 49854
(906) 341-3618

Shiawassee
208 N. Shiawassee
Corunna, MI 48817
(989) 743-2242

Tuscola
440 N. State
Caro, MI 48723
(989) 672-3780

Van Buren
212 Paw Paw St.
Paw Paw, MI 49079
(269) 657-8218

Washtenaw
P.O. Box 8645
Ann Arbor, MI 48107
(734) 222-6710

Wayne
201 City-County
Building
Detroit, MI 48226
(313) 224-6262

Wexford
437 E. Division
Cadillac, MI 49601
(231) 779-9450

Bureaus of Vital Statistics

Michigan Notaries are not authorized by law to certify copies of public records. Persons requesting certified copies of birth or death certificates should be referred to the appropriate public Bureau of Vital Statistics. The following state agencies can provide certified copies of birth and death records for persons who were born or have died in the respective states, as can certain local offices not listed here.

Alabama
Vital Records
Department of Public Health
P.O. Box 5625
Montgomery, AL 36103-5625

Alaska
Bureau of Vital Statistics
Dept. of Health &
Social Services
5441 Commercial Bl.
Juneau, AK 99801

Arizona
Office of Vital Records
Dept. of Health Services
P.O. Box 3887
Phoenix, AZ 85030-3887

Arkansas
Division of Vital Records
Department of Health
4815 West Markham Street, Slot 44
Little Rock, AR 72205-3867

California
Office of Vital Records
Department of Health Services
P.O. Box 997410, MS: 5103
Sacramento, CA 95899-7410

Colorado
Health Statistics
Department of Health
CHEIS-HS-A1
4300 Cherry Creek Drive South
Denver, CO 80246-1530

Connecticut
(Certified copies are not available from the state office. Requests must be made to the place where the event occurred.)

Delaware
Office of Vital Statistics
Division of Public Health
P.O. Box 637
Dover, DE 19903

District of Columbia
Department of Health
John A. Wilson Building
1350 Pennsylvania Avenue NW
Washington, DC 20004

Florida
Department of Health
Office of Vital Statistics
4052 Bald Cypress Way
Tallahassee, FL 32399-1701

Georgia
Vital Records
2600 Skyland Drive NE
Atlanta, GA 30319-3640

Hawaii
State Department of Health
Vital Statistics Section
P.O. Box 3378
Honolulu, HI 96801

Idaho
Department of Health and Welfare
Vital Statistics Unit
450 West State Street, 1st Floor
P.O. Box 83720
Boise, ID 83720

Illinois
Health Statistics
Department of Public Health
605 West Jefferson Street
Springfield, IL 62702-5097

Indiana
Vital Records Section
State Department of Health
2 North Meridian Street
Indianapolis, IN 46204

Iowa
Department of Public Health
Bureau of Vital Records
Lucas Office Building, 1st Floor
321 East 12th Street
Des Moines, IA 50319-0075

Kansas
Office of Vital Statistics
1000 SW Jackson Street, Suite 120
Topeka, KS 66612

Kentucky
Office of Vital Statistics
Department for Health Services
275 East Main Street-IE-A
Frankfort, KY 40621-0001

Louisiana
Vital Records Registry
Office of Public Health
325 Loyola Avenue
P.O. Box 60630
New Orleans, LA 70160

Maine
Department of Human Services
Vital Records
221 State Street, Station 11
11 State House Station
Augusta, ME 04333-0011

Maryland
Division of Vital Records
6550 Reisterstown Plaza
Reiserstown Road Plaza
Baltimore, MD 21215

Massachusetts
Vital Records and Statistics
150 Mt. Vernon Street, First Floor
Dorchester, MA 02125-3105

Michigan
Department of Community Health
3423 N. Martin Luther King Blvd.
P. O. Box 30721
Lansing, MI 48909

Minnesota
Department of Health
Attn: Office of the State Registrar
717 Delaware Street, SE
P.O. Box 9441
Minneapolis, MN 55440-9441

Mississippi
Vital Records
571 Stadium Drive
P.O. Box 1700
Jackson, MS 39215-1700

Missouri
Department of Health
Bureau of Vital Records
930 Wildwood
P.O. Box 570
Jefferson City, MO 65102

Montana
Office of Vital Statistics
Department of Public Health
P.O. Box 4210
111 North Sanders, Room 209
Helena, MT 59604

Nebraska
Vital Statistics
Department of Health
P.O. Box 95044
Lincoln, NE 68509-5044

Nevada
Division of Health / Vital Statistics
505 East King Street, Room #102
Carson City, NV 89701

New Hampshire
Bureau of Vital Records
29 Hazen Drive
Concord, NH 03301

New Jersey
Vital Statistics
Customer Service Unit
P.O. Box 370
Trenton, NJ 08625-0370

New Mexico
Vital Records and Health Statistics
P.O. Box 26110
1105 St. Francis Drive
Santa Fe, NM 87502

New York
Certification Unit
Vital Records Section
800 North Pearl Street, 2nd Floor
Menands, NY 12204

New York City
Office of Vital Records
NYC Department of Health and Mental Hygiene
125 Worth Street, CN4, Room 133
New York, NY 10013-4090

North Carolina
Vital Records
1903 Mail Service Center
Raleigh, NC 27699-1903

North Dakota
Division of Vital Records
600 East Boulevard Ave.
Department 301
Bismarck, ND 58505-0200

Ohio
Vital Statistics
246 North High Street
1st Floor
Columbus, OH 43216

Oklahoma
Vital Records Service
State Department of Health
1000 Northeast Tenth, Room 111
Oklahoma City, OK 73117

Oregon
Oregon Vital Records
800 NE Oregon Street, Ste 205
PO Box 14050
Portland, OR 97293

Pennsylvania
Vital Records
State Department of Health
101 S. Mercer Street
P.O. Box 1528
New Castle, PA 16101

Rhode Island
Office of Vital Records
Department of Health
3 Capitol Hill
Room 101
Providence, RI 02908-5097

South Carolina
Office of Vital Records
2600 Bull Street
Columbia, SC 29201

South Dakota
Department of Health
Vital Records
600 East Capitol Avenue
Pierre, SD 57501-2536

Tennessee
Vital Records
Central Services Building
1st Floor
421 5th Avenue North
Nashville, TN 37247

Texas
Bureau of Vital Statistics
Department of Health
P.O. Box 12040
Austin, TX 78711-2040

Utah
Vital Records & Statistics
Cannon Health Building
288 North 1460 West
P.O. Box 141012
Salt Lake City, UT 84114-1012

Vermont
Department of Health
Vital Records Section
108 Cherry Street
P.O. Box 70
Burlington, VT 05402-0070

Virginia
Office of Vital Records
P.O. Box 1000
Richmond, VA 23218

Washington
Department of Health
Center for Health Statistics
P.O. Box 9709
Olympia, WA 98507-9709

West Virginia
Vital Registration Office
350 Capitol Street, Room 165
Charleston, WV 25301-3701

Wisconsin
Vital Records
1 W. Wilson St., P.O. Box 309
Madison, WI 53701-0309

Wyoming
Vital Records Services
Hathaway Building
Cheyenne, WY 82002

American Samoa
Registrar of Vital Statistics
Vital Statistics Section
Government of American Samoa
Pago Pago, AS 96799

Guam
Department of Public Health
and Social Services
Government of Guam
P.O. Box 2816
Agana, GU M.I. 96932

Northern Mariana Islands
Commonwealth Recorder
Superior Court
Vital Records Section
P.O. Box 500307
Saipan, MP 96910

Panama Canal Zone
Vital Records Section
Passport Services
U.S. Dept. of State
1111 19th Street NW, Suite 510
Washington, DC, CZ 34011-2300

Puerto Rico
Department of Health
Demographic Registry
P.O. Box 11854
Fernández Juncos Station
San Juan, PR 00910

Virgin Islands (St. Croix)
Department of Health
Vital Statistics
Charles Harwood Memorial Complex
Christiansted, St. Croix, VI 00820

Virgin Islands (St. Thomas, St. John)
Dept. of Health, Vital Statistics
Old Municipal Hospital
St. Thomas, VI 00802

Hague Convention Nations

The nations listed on the following pages are parties to a treaty called the *Hague Convention Abolishing the Requirement of Legalization [Authentication] for Foreign Public Documents*, hereafter simply called the Hague Convention.

Treaty Simplifies Authentication. A Notary's signature on documents that are sent to these nations may be authenticated (verified as valid for the benefit of the recipient in the foreign nation) through attachment of a single authenticating certificate called an *apostille*. The *apostille* (French for "notation") is the only authenticating certificate necessary. Nations not subscribing to the Hague Convention may require as many as five or six separate authenticating certificates from different governmental agencies, domestic and foreign.

How to Request an *Apostille*. To obtain an *apostille*, anyone may mail the notarized document and $1 per notarized document (payable to the "State of Michigan) to:

By Regular Mail:
Michigan Dept. of State
Office of the Great Seal
7064 Crowner Blvd.
Lansing, MI 48918

Walk-in or Courier:
Michigan Dept. of State
Office of the Great Seal
Richard H. Austin Building 1st Flr.
430 W. Allegan Street
Lansing, MI 48915

An *apostille* must be specifically requested, and the nation to which the document will be sent must be indicated. It is not the Notary's responsibility to obtain an *apostille*; it is the responsibility of the party needing authentication.

Hague Convention Nations. The nations listed below participate in the Hague Convention. Footnotes reflect information most likely to be of interest to Notaries acting in the United States and its territories. Please note that some nations listed may not recognize the participation of every other nation listed. To verify recognition between nations, consult the Web site of the Hague Conference on Private International Law at http://www.hcch.net/index_en.php.

Albania
Andorra[13]
Antigua and Barbuda[13]
Argentina[1]
Armenia[13]
Australia
Austria
Azerbaijan[13]
Bahamas[13]
Barbados[13]
Belarus
Belgium[8]
Belize[13]
Bosnia and Herzegovina[2]
Botswana[13]
Brunei Darussalam[13]
Bulgaria
Cape Verde[13]
Colombia[13]
Cook Islands[13]
Croatia[2]
Cyprus
Czech Republic
Denmark[3]
Dominica[13]
Dominican Republic[13]
Ecuador
El Salvador[13]
Estonia
Fiji[13]
Finland
France[4]
Georgia[5]
Germany[8]
Greece
Grenada[13]
Honduras[13]
Hong Kong[6]
Hungary
Iceland
India
Ireland
Israel
Italy
Japan
Kazakhstan[13]
Latvia
Lesotho[13]
Liberia[8,13]
Liechtenstein[13]
Lithuania
Luxembourg
Macao[6]
Macedonia[2]
Malawi[13]
Malta
Marshall Islands[13]
Mauritius[13]
Mexico
Moldova[13]

1. Argentina does not recognize the extension of the Convention by the United Kingdom to the Malvinas (Falkland Islands), South Georgia, South Sandwich Islands and the Argentine Antarctic Sector (British Antarctic Territory). See n. 11.

2. The former Socialist Federal Republic of Yugoslavia was a party to the Convention. Only the successor states of Bosnia and Herzegovina, Croatia, the Republic of Macedonia, Montenegro, Serbia and Slovenia have confirmed that the Convention still applies.

3. The participation of Denmark does not extend to Greenland and the Faro Islands.

4. The participation of France is extended to the entire territory of the French Republic, including French Guyana, French Polynesia, Guadeloupe, Martinique, Mayotte, New Caledonia, Reunion, St. Barthelemy, St. Martin, St. Pierre and Miquelon, and Wallis and Futuna.

5.The participation of Georgia does not extend to Abkhazia and South Ossetia.

6. Hong Kong and Macao retained their status as Hague nations after control was returned to China on July 1, 1997 (Hong Kong) and December 20, 1999 (Macao).

Monaco
Mongolia[13]
Montenegro[2]
Namibia[13]
Netherlands[9]
New Zealand[7]
Niue[13]
Norway
Panama
Peru
Poland
Portugal[10]
Romania
Russian Federation
Saint Kitts and Nevis[13]
Saint Lucia[13]
Saint Vincent and the Grenadines[13]
Samoa[13]
San Marino[13]
Sao Tome e Principe[13]
Serbia[2]
Seychelles[13]
Slovakia
Slovenia[2]
South Africa
South Korea
Spain
Suriname
Swaziland[13]
Sweden
Switzerland
Tonga[13]
Trinidad and Tobago[13]
Turkey
Ukraine
United Kingdom[1,11]
United States[8,12]
Vanuatu[13]
Venezuela

Inquiries. Persons having questions about the *Hague Convention Abolishing the Requirement of Legalization for Foreign Public Documents* may address their inquiries to:

U.S. Dept. of State
Authentication Office
518 23rd Street N.W.
State Annex 1
Washington, DC 20520
(202) 647-5002

7. The participation of New Zealand does not extend to Tokelau.

8. The Convention does not apply between Liberia and the United States, Belgium or Germany.

9. The participation of the Netherlands is extended to Aruba and the Netherlands Antilles.

10. The participation of Portugal is extended to the entire territory of the Republic of Portugal, including the Azores and Madeira.

11. The participation of the United Kingdom of Great Britain and Northern Ireland is extended to Anguilla, Bermuda, British Antarctic Territory, British Virgin Islands, Cayman Islands, Falkland Islands, Gibraltar, Guernsey, Isle of Man, Jersey, Montserrat, St. Helena and Turks and Caicos Islands.

12. The United States includes American Samoa, District of Columbia, Guam, Northern Mariana Islands, Puerto Rico and U.S. Virgin Islands.

13. This nation is not a member of the Hague Conference on Private International Law but is a party to the *Hague Convention Abolishing the Requirement of Legalization for Foreign Public Documents.*

About the NNA

Since 1957, the National Notary Association — a nonprofit educational organization — has served the nation's Notaries Public with a wide variety of instructional programs and services.

As the country's clearinghouse for information on Notary laws, customs and practices, the NNA educates Notaries through publications, seminars, webinars, online training, annual conferences, its website and a Notary Information Service Hotline that offers immediate answers to specific questions about notarization.

The Association is perhaps most widely known as the preeminent source of information for and about Notaries. NNA works include the following:

- *The National Notary*, a magazine for NNA members featuring how-to articles and practical tips on notarizing

- *Notary Bulletin*, an online newsletter that keeps NNA members and customers up to date on developments affecting Notaries, especially new state laws and regulations

- *Sorry, No Can Do!* series, four volumes that help Notaries explain to signers and bosses why some requests for notarizations are improper and cannot be accommodated

- *U.S. Notary Reference Manual*, an invaluable resource for any person relying upon the authenticity and correctness of legal documents

- *Notary Public Practices & Glossary*, a definitive reference book on notarial procedures and widely hailed as the Notary's bible

- *State Notary Law Primers*, short guidebooks that explain a state's Notary statutes in easy-to-understand language

- *The Notary Public Code of Professional Responsibility*, a comprehensive and detailed code of ethical and professional conduct for Notaries

- *The Model Notary Act*, prototype legislation conceived in 1973 and updated in 1984, 2002 and 2010 by an NNA-recruited panel of secretaries of state, legislators and attorneys, and regularly used by state legislatures in revising their Notary laws

- *Notary Law & Practice: Cases & Materials*, the definitive and one-of-a-kind text for teaching Notary law to law students in schools and to attorneys in Minimum Continuing Education Seminars (MCLE), discussing every major judicial decision affecting the Notary's duties

- *Notary Signing Agent Training Course*, a manual covering every aspect of signing agent procedures that prepares candidates for the Notary Signing Agent Certification Examination developed by the NNA

- Public-service pamphlets informing the general public about the function of a Notary, including *What Is A Notary Public?* printed in English and Spanish

In addition, the NNA offers the highest quality professional tools, including official seals and stamps, embossers, recordkeeping journals, thumbprinting devices and notarial certificates.

Though dedicated primarily to educating and assisting Notaries, the NNA devotes part of its resources to helping lawmakers draft effective Notary statutes and to informing the public about the Notary's vital role in modern society. ■

Index

Page numbers listed in **bold** indicate where the most complete information on a subject can be found. *Italics* indicate pages where the statutes and state-published information pertaining to a subject are located.

NOTES

NOTES

NOTES